The Difficult Years of Survival

His Holiness Pope Shenoudah III,
the Pontiff Who Brought Honor
to the Coptic Church

The Difficult Years of Survival

A Short Account of the History of the Coptic Church

Fouad Guirguis

VANTAGE PRESS
New York / Washington / Atlanta
Los Angeles / Chicago

"The Third Letter of Cyril to Nestorius," "Appeal of Theo-
doret to Leo," "Flavian's Appeal to Leo," and "Theodoret
Complains to Dioscorus of Alexandria" are printed from
Creeds, Councils and Controversies, by J. Stevenson, with
permission from The Society for Promoting Christian
Knowledge.

FIRST EDITION

Copyright © 1985 by Fouad Guirguis

Published by Vantage Press, Inc.
516 West 34th Street, New York, New York 10001

Manufactured in the United States of America
ISBN: 0-533-05937-2

Library of Congress Catalog No.: 83-90921

A Spanish poet wrote: "Traveler, there is no path; paths are made by walking." Will the Copts ever understand the meaning of these words?

Contents

Introduction

The Difficult Years of Survival is a short account of the history of the Coptic Church during the decisive years A.D. 499 to 451 and its role in the councils of Ephesus II and Chalcedon, which determined the fate of the Universal Church and the integrity of the Byzantine Empire. Writing this book has not been an easy task because of the complex nature of the topics discussed, especially as the Roman Catholic historians have deliberately shrouded the Coptic Church and its dogmas in a veil of Eutychianism.

The main religious figures that influenced the events during the years 449 to 451 were Pope Dioscorus of Alexandria, Archbishops Flavian of Constantinople, Domnus of Antioch, Juvenal of Jerusalem, and Leo of Rome. After the Council of Chalcedon, the Catholic theologians labeled Pope Dioscorus a heretic and Archbishop Leo a saint.

In this book I have analytically reexamined the minutes and proceedings of the councils of Ephesus II and Chalcedon, a study that revealed that Archbishop Leo of Rome was a man who vigorously pursued power and supremacy over the Universal Church at any cost. In fact, Archbishop Leo, who claimed to bear witness to Christ's own mind inherited through the Apostle Peter, followed every illegal path to crush Saint Dioscorus of Alexandria.

At the Council of Chalcedon, Leo arranged for the reckless and unfounded accusations that were directed against Pope Dioscorus. Interestingly, there is no definite accusation against Pope Dioscorus in the vague resolution adopted by some of the bishops at Chalcedon to depose him. In addition, Archbishop Anatolius of Constantinople, who was one of the chief participants at Chalcedon and an ally of Leo, had stated on more than one occasion that Pope Dioscorus has not been excommunicated on a question of faith but because he excommunicated Lord Bishop Leo and did not respond to threefold summons.

From exile, Pope Dioscorus sent pastoral letters to Secondinus and the monks of Enaton. The Copts, monks and laymen until today consider that the two letter of Saint Dioscorus were sent to them personally to strengthen their faith in a time of tribulation. To the Copts, the two pastoral letters by Saint Dioscorus are equivalent to the resurrection letters sent to them by his predecessor Saint Athanasius of Alexandria while he was in exile.

Later, Archbishop Leo claimed that his tome was accepted and welcomed by all the bishops who attended the Council of Chalcedon. Regardless of the fact that the tome of Leo cannot be considered a serious document that substantially contributed towards the understanding of the well-established Christian faith, at Chalcedon the tome was approved by a committee of 23 bishops out of about 360 who were present at the council.

With his tome, Archbishop Leo had interfered in matters that did not concern him, as the theological dialogue was between Alexandria and Antioch, the main two schools of Christological thought at the time. In this context, it is interesting to note that the formulary of reunion between Saint Cyril I of Alexandria and Bishop John of Antioch was arranged without even consulting Rome.

In brief, Archbishop Leo had made the council of Chalcedon a *political den* and converted the spiritual hierarchy of the See of Rome into a *political organization* with devastating consequences. Some of the far-reaching consequences were the first schism in the Universal Church, the ascending of men like Formosus (891–69), Calixtus III (1455–58), and his nephew Alexander VI (1492–1503) of the Borgia family to the See of Rome and the second separation in the Church. The Greek Orthodox Church severed its ties with the Church of Rome during the papacy of another Leo, Leo IX (1049–54) of Rome.

The second topic discussed, even though briefly, is the contemporary relationship between the Coptic Church and the government of Egypt, which was severely strained by the erratic and irresponsible political maneuvers of the late president Mr. Sadat. In order to secure a lifetime presidency, Mr. Sadat addressed the religious instinct of the Muslim majority and aligned himself with the anarchical concepts and activities of radical Muslim societies. Mr. Sadat's gamble ended on October 6, 1981, leaving behind an Egyptian society struck by poverty, illiteracy, and chronic religious problems.

Finally, it must be emphasized that this book is not an attack on the Catholic Church or its dogmas, nor on Archbishop Leo. Rather, the primary concern of this book is a rational exegesis of an important chapter in the history of the Church from a different perspective, in the light of reinvestigating the events of 449 and 451 that led to the first schism in the one body of the Church of Christ.

Munich, 1984

The Difficult Years of Survival

The Copts of Egypt

Thou makest the earth shine like fine copper,
The dead rise up to see thee,
They breathe the air and they look upon
thy face when Aton shineth in the horizon.

The ancient Egyptians who uttered these beautiful words depicting the one God, Aton, were converted to Christianity by Saint Mark the Evangelist. Thus the Coptic Orthodox Church of the See of Alexandria was established in A.D. 61. The Christians of Egypt are often referred to as Copts. The Arabs deformed the Greek word Aigyptos—derived from the hieroglyphic *Ha Ka patah*—to *el Gipty*, which was further deformed in the English language to *Copts*.

Christianity did not spread into a religious vacuum in Egypt. Well-established cults—for example, the Osiris cult, the Amon cult, and remnants of the Aton cult—already existed alongside others of Greek origin. Nevertheless, by the time of Pope Theophilous the Great, who occupied the throne of Saint Mark from A.D. 384–412, the entire Egyptian population had converted to the new religion, Christianity. Endowed with a rich heritage, the Church of Alexandria provided the Christian world with great theologians such as Clement and Origen of Alexandria, Popes Athanasius, Cyril I, Dioscorus, Antony, and Pachomius, the founders of monastic life.

Despite the long tradition of religion and culture, the Copts did not enjoy a pleasant life. The heaviest toll of martyrdom took place during the time of Diolectian (A.D. 303) and during the purge of the Orthodox Christians of Egypt by the Arian and Chalcedonian bishops, who were appointed by different emperors to the See of Alexandria.

Psychological abuse was also characteristic of this period. The Copts were distressed to see their marvelous

1

Egyptian heritage, manifested in the library of Alexandria, destroyed by fire. Historically, it is well documented that Amer ben el Aas, the leader of the Arab invasion forces in Egypt, received orders from Khalif Amer ben el Khatab: "If these books [of the library of Alexandria] contain nothing more than that which is written in el Koran, they are useless; if they contain anything that contradicts Koran, they are pernicious; in either case burn them!" The books were numerous enough to provide six months' fuel for the public baths of Alexandria.

During the stormy years of the foreign occupation of Egypt (e.g., Byzantine, Arab (A.D. 640), and Turkish (1517), the Coptic Church not only strove to keep the faith in the heart of its followers, but also struggled for its very existence. History books are filled with accounts of the barbaric means by which Ommyades, Abbasides, Mamlouks, and Turks suppressed Christianity and purged Christians in Egypt. The Copts, even though significantly reduced in number and status, looked upon their national archbishop of Alexandria, whom they elect, as their religious and secular leader. The perplexed conquerors were unwilling or unable to understand the loyalty the Copts showed to their Pope. This is not only because the succession to the See of Alexandria remained uninterrupted since A.D. 61, but it is also the sequel to eight thousand years of cultural tradition in Egypt.

The ancient Egyptian culture aimed at life after death. The bodies of the deceased had to be preserved (the mummification process), with the intent of keeping the physical features intact as much as possible, so that the returning souls could recognize their own bodies for the resurrection. Thus the mixing of chemicals and salts was initiated. Statues carved out of solid rocks and marvelous drawings on the walls of the tomb or the sarcophagus resembling the deceased were necessary so that the returning soul could find rest in the event that the mummified corpse did decay.

Prayers, poetry, philosophy, and monasticism were also the natural products of the ancient Egyptians' infinite search for the power beneath the natural phenomenon, i.e., God. Consequently, wisdom was in the person of the high priest. Therefore, the authority of the high priest was considered second to the Pharaoh. Nevertheless, the spiritual authority of the high priest and the executive power of the pharaoh never overlapped.[1] Logically, the ancient Egyptians regarded the high priest with esteem and respect, as the very man who linked them to the Creator's almighty power. The ancient Egyptians looked upon the high priest to guide them in their spiritual life and everyday life when the political sovereignty of the Third Kingdom collapsed with the advance of the Persians, Greeks, and Romans. To them, the high priest represented the soul of Egypt; he was the "Egyptian" selected by the priests as a counterforce to foreign rule. The attitude of the ancient Egyptians was transferred quantitatively in A.D. 61, when the Pope of Alexandria assumed the mantle of the high priest of Christianity. To the Copts, the Pope of Alexandria traditionally represented national dignity, and still does so today, and this became historical inevitability.

The Dilemma of the Copts of Egypt

The Coptic dilemma is a very sensitive and difficult issue to relate to readers. The various confessions of the Western world look upon the Copts as "the heretics of Alexandria" or the "Eutychians"! In their home, Egypt, the Copts feel they are discriminated against at almost

3

every level of daily life by the different governments of the 1952 coup d'etat colonels.

Before Anwar Sadat's death, his government practiced the policy of dividing Egypt into separate communities (Muslims versus Copts) by coordinating its efforts with Muslim fundamentalist groups to isolate the Copts from Egyptian Society. The Copts also feel that every possible effort has been made by the fundamentalists to assimilate them, their religion, their identity, and their culture into the Muslim masses.

Logically, the question is how the Copts reached such a desperate situation on April 2, 1980, when the Pope of Alexandria and the bishops reported a long list of incidents directed against Coptic individuals and the Church buildings, which were ravaged by mobs, namely:

1. The ravaging of the church in Nazlet Ali (constituency of Gahinah, Sugah).
2. The ravaging of the Church of the Holy Virgin (El-Betakh, region of Sugah).
3. The ravaging of the church in El-Awaisah (Samalut).
4. The ravaging of the Church of Itsa (Faium).
5. The attack on the Episcopal See of Assiut.
6. The attack on the convent of El-Fakhuri (Isna).
7. The Christmas Eve, 1980, bombing of two churches in Alexandria, the Church of Saint George in Gheit El-Inab and the Church of Saint George in Sporting.
8. The August 31, 1978, attack of fundamentalist mobs on the houses, fields, and shops of the Christians in the town of Tewfikiah (El-Meniah). Encouraged by the passive attitude of the town-police, the mobs on the second day attacked the Christians, put the Coptic males in chains, raped Coptic women and young Coptic girls, and mercilessly beat young Coptic boys. In

4

hospitals, doctors refused to attend to the injured Copts, and many were left bleeding to death. Minister Ghabrial El-Mutugali (seventy years old) was murdered. Mrs. Hineihah Qullini (seventy years old) was murdered. Badari Naguib, an eleven-year-old boy, was also killed.

9. The killing of two young Christians of Menschat, Upper Egypt, murdered because of their refusal to convert to Islam.

10. The kidnapping and rape of Christian girls of Assiut, El-Miniah, Beni-Suef, Alexandria, El-Mataraiah, and Cairo, who were also forced to marry Muslims and renounce Christianity.

11. The consistent attacks upon Coptic students in the halls of residence of Alexandria University.

With all of his insecurities, Mr. Sadat interpreted the 1980 Easter move of Pope Shenoudah III against the tyranny of the Muslim fanatics as an attack on his own person.[2] The courageous move of the Pope stunned Sadat and haunted him day and night. This was manifested in Sadat's personal attack on the Pope on every possible occasion during the year 1981. The undivided support given to the Pope by the poor Copts was magnificent.

However, the initially successful papal move ended in a complete disaster, as Sadat very cleverly managed to create a class struggle between the Copts themselves during this critical time. While the majority of the Copts, the poor, supported the Pope, as mentioned above, the rich Copts, worried about their government privileges, opposed the Pope. Even though the Copts have a good sense of survival, they failed to pose as a coherent body at this crucial moment.

By the end of 1981, Mr. Sadat came to the realization

that the Copts regarded him as one of the very many corrupt Mamlouks who governed Egypt, whereas they regarded Shenoudah III as one of the very few great Coptic Popes to occupy the throne of Saint Mark. In his zeal, Mr. Sadat forgot that Copts still recalled his activities in 1940–50 as an assassin, when he was an active member of both the Muslim brotherhood and the Nazi movement of "Misr el Fattah" led by Mr. Ahmed Hussein. Every Copt knew that Mr. Sadat had decided to neutralize the Pope.

As expected, the situation did not stop at this point, but events proceeded quickly during 1981. Sadat, in co-operation with the Muslim extremist societies, deliberately escalated the war against the person of the Pope, trying to create a gap between the Pope and the poor Coptic people. Many Copts, especially women and children, lost their lives in this state-engineered sectarian strife that erupted in the underprivileged area of Zawia el Hammra. Mr. Sadat took advantage of the situation by declaring his decision to revoke the government recognition of Shenoudah III as the Pope of Alexandria on September 5, 1981, and to arrest about two to three thousand of his political opponents. In brief, the whole atmosphere in Egypt was pregnant with hate, which broke into the ugly assassination of October 6, 1981.

Even though they disregarded Sadat's decision and still acknowledged the authority of Pope Shenoudah as the supreme head of the Coptic Church and their spiritual leader, the Copts were unable to shed the feeling that they were very isolated in their own home of Egypt. Moreover, they felt that the head of the state interfered in their private religious affairs, a fact that reminded them of their grandfathers' suffering during the long, grueling years of the Mamlouks' and Turks' rule in Egypt.

6

The chain reaction of historical events that led to such a sad situation, the decline of the Coptic cultural identity, was initiated at the Council of Chalcedon, A.D. 451, and was later reaffirmed during the long years of the Arab occupation of Egypt.

The severity with which the Copts were persecuted by the Chalcedonians and the Arabs resulted in:

1. The Coptic paradox: a major transformation in the personality and character of the Egyptian population who preferred to remain Copts, and
2. A massive conversion to Islamic religion.

In brief, the paradox of the Coptic personality manifests itself by its deep sense of survival versus its failure to pose as an effective and coherent public body. This phenomenon is especially prevalent during the time of crisis, when the Coptic existence is threatened.[3]

Let us start from the beginning.

The Road to Chalcedon

To facilitate the reader's understanding of our thesis, the three major Christian dogmas of the time written about are briefly described below. However, we should stress that this book does not address itself to the theological differences between these three dogmas, but rather to the legality and the proceeding of the councils of Ephesus II and Chalcedon.

The Alexandrian Christology: Explained by Cyril I at the First Council of Ephesus and Defended by Dioscorus at the Second Council of Ephesus

This Christology is shared by the Churches of Alexandria and Rome, as shown in the common declaration of His Holiness Pope Shenoudah III and Pope Paul VI of Rome May 10, 1973. The declaration confirms: "We confess one faith in the One Triune God, the Divinity of the Only Begotten Son of God, the Second Person of the Holy Trinity, the World of God, the effulgence of his Glory and the express image of His substance, who for us was incarnate, assuming for Himself a real body with a rational soul and who shared with us our humanity but without sin. We confess that our Lord and God and Savior and King of us all, Jesus Christ, is a perfect God with respect to His Divinity, perfect man with respect to His humanity. In Him, Divinity is united with His humanity in a real, perfect union without mingling, without commixtion, without confusion, without alteration, without division, without separation. His Divinity did not separate from His humanity for an instant, not for the twinkling of an eye. He Who is God, eternal and invisible, became visible in the flesh, and took upon Himself the form of a servant. In Him are preserved all the properties of Divinity and all the properties of humanity, together in a real, perfect, indivisible and inseparable union."

The Nestorian Dogma

This is belief in two natures after the Incarnation with separation and division of the humanity and Divinity of the Incarnate Word and considered a heresy at the Councils of Ephesus I, Ephesus II, and Chalcedon.

The Dogma of Eutyches

It was considered a revival of Apollinarius and Mani's thoughts of Christianity and one nature after the Incarnation. It states that: The human body of Christ is totally confused, mixed and absorbed with His Divinity. Thus, the body of Christ is not of our nature. This heresy was condemned by the four major Sees of Christianity: Alexandria, Antioch, Rome, and Constantinople.

In A.D. 444, Cyril I of Rakotis[4] died. Dioscorus,[4] his archdeacon, succeeded him. At Constantinople, Flavian, the patriarch, succeeded Proclus. Flavian had a very weak personality, which was dominated by an arch Nestorian, Eusebius of Dorylaeum, a man determined to revive the Nestorian heresy at any cost. In turn, these two men were joined by Ibas of Edessa, Theodoret of Cyrrhos, Basil of Seleucia, and other bishops from the East, who seized the opportunity to propagate Nestorianism in the person of Eutyches, the archimandrite from Constantinople. In his zeal, Eutyches went to the opposite extreme in reacting to the heresy of Nestorius. He claimed that the Incarnate Word Christ the Lord was a man but that His flesh was not consubstantial with ours. The new heresy of Eutyches could have extinguished itself, especially since its formulation was clearly anti-Nicene and anti–Ephesian I, something that Rome and Alexandria would have never accepted.

A regional council in Constantinople (A.D. 448) was quickly convened, with Flavian presiding and Eusebius of Dorylaeum, the old enemy of Eutyches, as his prosecutor. At that council, every bishop was concerned with his interpretation and pronunciation of the Christian faith, which was definitely far from the standard Orthodoxy as defined and accepted in Ephesus I, on the basis of the three letters of Cyril I of Rakotis to Nestorius of Constantinople (especially the third letter with the twelve anathemas).

Basil of Seleucia, without any criticism from the convened bishops, amended his statement of faith: "I adore One Christ, acknowledged in two natures after the Incarnation" a statement that Nestorius himself would have used to express his faith. Eutyches, the "frenzied blasphemer," as Eusebius described him, made every possible attempt not to attend the council—once because he had vowed not to leave his cloister, a second time because he objected to Eusebius as his personal enemy, and a third time due to illness. After the seventh summons, Eutyches attended the council accompanied by a patrician whom Emperor Theodosius appointed to protect Eutyches from the potential violence that Eusebius could inspire among Nestorian partisans.

There is no doubt that Eutyches committed himself to the heresies of Apollinarius and Mani. However, the regional council at Constantinople was unable to conduct a reasonable dialogue with Eutyches. On the contrary, the bishops tried to force Eutyches to accept the idea of the Nestorian heresy, i.e., the concept of his arch enemy Nestorius: Two natures after the Incarnation. Eutyches refused.[5] Furthermore, this cunning old man, Eutyches, evaded the questions of his accusers and, when forced, gave very evasive answers. The following dialogue is self-explanatory:

Flavian asked Eutyches if the flesh of Christ was consubstantial with ours. Eutyches replied:

As I acknowledge it is the body of the Lord, I would not say that the flesh of the Lord is a human flesh. I have said that His body is human and that God became incarnate from the Virgin, and, if I have to say it, [His body] is from the Virgin, I would say it, Your Holiness. However, I would not say that the Only Begotten Son of God, the Lord of

10

Heaven and Earth, whom I acknowledge God and King
with the Father, who is with Him in glory, is consubstantial
with our nature, and would be denying the Son of God if
I have said so!

Then he was asked, "Do you acknowledge that the
Lord is from the Virgin and has two natures after the
Incarnation?"

Eutyches' answer was: "I confess of the two natures
before the Incarnation, but after the union I acknowledge
one nature."

"If you do not believe in two natures after the union,
then you believe in the confusion, mixing and mingling
of the two natures?" Basil of Seleucia asked. No response
was forthcoming from Eutyches.

Eusebius of Dorylaeum asked Eutyches twice, "Does
the archimandrite acknowledge two natures after the Incarnation and that Christ was of one substance with ours?"
At that point, the bishops did not wait to hear Eutyches'
answer and excommunicated him.

Eutyches did not agree with his excommunication and
complained to Emperor Theodosius and Bishop Leo of
Rome and many other bishops. Bishop Leo wrote to Flavian asking him to grant Eutyches mercy. Leo himself
wrote to Eutyches praising his Orthodox faith and de-
nouncing those reviving Nestorianism![6] (Also see appendix, p. 41.)

Needless to say, Leo of Rome, while sending his fath-
erly letter to Eutyches, was fully aware that the archimandrite had been excommunicated and was deposed by
Flavian, Eusebius, Basil, and others at the regional council
of Constantinople. Leo also received a letter from Flavian
in which he defended his deeds at the council. Knowing
Leo and his burning desire to establish the supremacy of
the Roman See, Leo seized this opportunity to write his

11

definition of Christology in what was known later as the *Tome of Leo!* Futhermore, it is interesting to note that in his letter to Emperor Theodosius, Leo made the pronouncement that the accusation against Eutyches submitted to the regional council of Constantinople by Eusebius was not sound enough to permit his deposition and condemnation.[7]

In brief, Eutyches accused Flavian and his group of Nestorianism. In turn, Flavian anathematized Eutyches as a Mani and Apollinarian blasphemer, while each side chose the words of the Copts Saint Cyril I and Saint Athanasius to support his argument of Christology. Thus, the universal Church was heading for religious havoc, especially after Leo of Rome made his tome known. Emperor Theodosius realized that the stability of his empire was at stake once again, because of the religious melancholy that erupted between Eutyches and Flavian and the ambition of Leo.

To avoid foregone consequences, Emperor Theodosius ordered the archbishops of Rakotis, Rome, Constantinople, Antioch, and Jerusalem to hold a council in Ephesus in order to eliminate religious problems that would definitely cause political strife in his empire. As can be seen from the emperor's declaration (see appendix, p. 41), Archbishop Dioscorus of Rakotis received the emperor's decree, as did all other archbishops. Therefore, the claim of the Roman Catholic historians that Dioscorus had influenced the emperor to call for a new ecumenical council is incorrect.

Furthermore, we can conclude the following from the emperor's letter to Dioscorus:

1. The emperors of the East and the West were aware of the danger resulting from the eruption of conflicts and

feuds over the issue of the nature of Christ, a question that had already been settled by Saint Cyril I of Rakotis at Ephesus I, in A.D. 431. On this basis, Nestorius, the archbishop of Constantinople, was condemned and then deposed.

A doctrinal dispute between Eutyches and Flavian flared up once again. The emperors called for another council, Ephesus II, in an attempt to resolve the issue and to implement the canons of Nicaea and Ephesus I.

2. From the experience of Ephesus I,[8] the two emperors ordered Theodoret of Cyrrhos, a leading Nestorianizer from Antioch, to confine himself to his diocese to avoid disrupting the proceedings of the council and ultimately destroying peace in the provinces of the empire with the potential division of the empire into two irreconcilable religious sects.

Nevertheless, the emperors treated Theodoret fairly by giving him an opportunity to repudiate his Nestorian teachings, as they left it to the council to deliberate with Theodoret if necessary. In this regard, Theodosius was a farsighted Emperor.

Theodosius' expectations came true in A.D. 451, when Emperor Marcian and his wife, Pulcheria, allowed the Nestorian bishops, Basil and Theodoret, to dominate the proceedings of the Council of Chalcedon. Separation took place. The empire's strength was impaired by its division into the Orthodox East and Catholic West. Therefore, the facile disintegration and the fall of the southern part of the Byzantine Empire, Egypt, Syria, and Palestine, into the hands of the Arabs in A.D. 640 should not be that surprising at all.

3. Cyril I of Rakotis laid down the foundation of the Universal-Orthodox Christology at Ephesus I, A.D. 431, according to the Bible, apostolic teachings, and the

writings of his Coptic predecessor Athanasius. Naturally, Theodosius had to select a man from the same Orthodox "school of thought" to chair Ephesus II. Inevitably, that man was Saint *Dioscorus* of Rakotis, the successor to Cyril I. The emperor was very judicious in appointing Juvenal of Jerusalem and the bishop of Cappadocia Caesarea[9] to preside with Dioscorus, so that no Bishop of these major Sees would dominate the proceedings and prejudice the outcome, and later may have had the grounds to claim the general supremacy over the others. Saint Dioscorus gained a formidable enemy in the person Leo of Rome. His jealousy over the appointment of Dioscorus as council chairman knew no bounds. He refused to attend the council and sent his legates instead.

The Second Ephesian Council, A.D. 449

Historically, this council was an extension of the Ephesian I held A.D. 431, chaired by Cyril I. Theologically, Ephesus II neither formulated nor defined creeds, but rather adhered to the canons established by the two Egyptians, Athanasius and Cyril I, in Nicaea and Ephesus I respectively.

At the opening session of Ephesus II, Dioscorus made the above point quite clear by declaring: "To satisfy everyone's conscience and thus supporting the faith and eliminate the present conflict, we adhere to the faith of the Fathers of Nicaea and Ephesus."

We have no doubt that the definition of the Christian universal faith was very clear in the mind of Dioscorus as he made the relationship between Ephesus I and II obvious from the very beginning: "It may be said two councils, but they have the same and one faith." To that, the bishops responded: "The fathers have ideally defined everything; he who opposes, let him be anathema. No one adds or omits." Again the words of Dioscorus were decisive and firm: "Because God hears your voices and accepts them, you too accept what is graceful to God. Let him be anathema he who investigates decrees or preaches contrary to what has been decided upon earlier by the Fathers who convened in the city of Nicaea and those who met here [Ephesus]."

The bishops were moved by the words of the archbishop of Rakotis confirming the Orthodox faith of the Fathers (Nicaea and Ephesus I). They cheered him: "Long live Dioscorus, the archbishop and protector of the great faith." Dioscorus continued his sermon: "I would like to say the following. If a man is abusive to another, which in itself is frightening, we pray to God for him. But if a man is offensive to God, who would dare and pray for his sake? And because the Holy Spirit was in the midst of the Fathers' council [Nicaea and Ephesus I] and defined the faith, whoever tries to distort their definition is scurrilous to the grace of God. No one changes what has been decided." The gathering of the bishops again expressed their joyfulness: "This is the voice of the Holy Spirit, O guardian of faith, O protector of faith, Dioscorus the archbishop."

The letter of the two emperors to the council (see appendix, p. 43) was read to the bishops by John, Dioscorus' scribe, thereby signaling the beginning of the deliberation of the conflict between Eutyches and Flavian, which would decide the fate of several of the Eastern bishops who embraced Nestorian dogmas.

In analyzing the emperor's letter to the council, we can envision three critical points attracting the attention of the bishops (see appendix, pp. 43 and 44), namely:

1. A further confirmation of the Orthodox faith on the doctrinal foundations laid down at Nicaea and Ephesus I.
2. The bishops had to settle the Flavian-Eutyches conflict. We also note that the emperors showed their dislike of Flavian's conduct, which endangered the peace of their subjects.
3. Removal of bishops with Nestorian inclinations from their offices.

Point 1 was addressed by the dialogue that took place between Saint Dioscorus of Rakotis and the rest of the bishops. They agreed that no Orthodox believer should deviate from, add, omit, or preach contrary to the ideal, universal, and Orthodox formulation of the Fathers of Nicaea and Ephesus I.

The council then moved to consider the genuineness of the faith of several bishops and the infamous Flavian-Eutyches feud.

At this point, it is worth mentioning that Leo, the archbishop of Rome, had written to Emperor Theodosius and the bishops of Ephesus II, clearly siding with Flavian from the standpoint of dogma. That was a tactical mistake on the part of Leo. Not only did he contravene the efforts of Emperor Theodosius to bring peace and tranquility to the nation by removing militant Nestorian bishops from their offices, but he also intervened openly with the Fathers of Ephesus II by influencing them to favor Flavian and the Nestorian group of the Synod of Constantinople, A.D. 448, even before the Fathers had the chance to read the minutes of that synod and formulate their own opinion. That was typical of Leo who used theological conflicts to accomplish worldly ends.[10] The irony is that the three letters of Cyril I to Nestorius, in particular the third one with the Twelve Anathema (see appendix, p. 55), were accepted by Leo at Chalcedon! This leads us to a serious question: Was Leo, disregarding his political skills, intellectually able to differentiate the subtleties of different Christian dogmas? Most of the statements in Leo's Tome were extracted from one of Augustine's sermons and from a letter from Bishop Gaudentius of Brescia.[11]

Upon careful reading of the minutes of the council of Ephesus II, published by Rome in 1694, we can clearly see that Dioscorus and Juvenal of Jerusalem followed a very rational approach in dealing with the disputes, e.g., they examined the subject with the Fathers of the council and read the minutes of previous councils that were related to the present conflict. When the prelates fully understood the given doctrinal debate, discussion followed, and then the president of the council or one of his two associates asked the prelates to declare their judgment. This procedure caused protracted, in-depth, intense debates among the zealous proponents of conflicting ideas, such that, on several occasions, the discussion broke into a furious match of shouting. Unfortunately, we have to realize that shouting and violence were not unusual, as the Council of Chalcedon had witnessed brutal physical violence and great injustices against the person of Pope Dioscorus.

Let us see if the Fathers at Ephesus II, under difficult circumstances, adhered to the Christian spirit in dealing with the Nestorian bishops of the East and with the two most sensitive issues examined: that of Flavian of Constantinople and Eutyches and that of Domnus of Antioch.

The three bishops (Ibas of Edessa, his nephew Daniel, and his cousin) turned out to be zealous Nestorians.[12] The case of Ibas and his relatives was studied carefully by the Fathers at Ephesus II. Many documents incriminating Ibas were submitted to the council by civilians, presbyters, and some monks of Edessa. It is interesting to note that neither Domnus of Antioch nor the Roman legates attended this session. When these documents were read to the Fathers, who realized their grave, unorthodox consequences, they asked Dioscorus to submit the minutes of this case to the emperor. Then a wave of uneasiness and restlessness spread into the council's hall, to which Dioscorus quickly responded: "Please secure peace to the council. It is written: in gentleness we listen to the wise. We should not shout otherwise we give the chance to the opposition to blame us. I know of your deep love of God. It is impressive that bishops, presbyters, and civilians would struggle for the sake of faith; we should strictly adhere to order, however."

In the second session, the Fathers at Ephesus II unanimously excommunicated Ibas after the bishops of Rakotis, Jerusalem, and Cappadocia and another eighteen leading bishops made their judgment known. Also, they condemned four other bishops of lesser importance, including the cousin and nephew of Ibas.

As for Theodoret of Cyrrhos, he was very active in preaching Nestorianism within Antioch. Theodoret's unorthodox activity stirred political unrest in the Oriental provinces of the Eastern Empire. (See the letters of Dioscorus to Domnus, appendix, p. 66.) As a result, the emperors did not recommend Theodoret's participation in Ephesus II and issued an edict confining him to his diocese. According to the council minutes published in Rome in 1694, Juvenal of Jerusalem initiated Theodoret's case by giving permission to a priest from Antioch to read to the council the documents incriminating Theodoret, e.g., Theodoret's Tomes against Ephesus I and Cyril I of Rakotis to Edessa and Antioch. These letters not only defended the dogma of Nestorius and his master, Theodore of Mopsuestia, but also contained degrading remarks about a famed Coptic national, Cyril I of Rakotis.

The bishops were stunned by what they heard and considered the evidence sufficient to excommunicate Theodoret; they reasoned that if they had to accept him, they might as well accept Nestorius himself. After the Fathers freely put forth their points of view, Dioscorus judged that:

> Theodoret was and still is an evil. He is propagating his heresies and did not renunciate his evil. Because of his unrighteous deeds, he tried to bewilder our Christ-loving kings through cunning ways and to swerve their consciences with the false doctrine. As a result, our kings were perplexed and caused the loss of many souls, and unsettled the whole of the Eastern Church. He sowed the seeds of an evil dogma and did not spare any effort to spread it among the innocent. He dared to preach and write against the earlier decrees, especially those Orthodox principles laid down by Saint Cyril I, the archbishop of happy memory. Therefore, let him be estranged from priesthood completely and the dignity of the bishopric office. He is forbidden from communion with the believers. Let all the pious bishops know that after this ecumenical council's judgment against Theodoret, he who dares to shelter him, share his table, or even talk to him has to justify his deeds to the Lord on the day of judgment, and be condemned for challenging a decision of this holy ecumenical council. This judgment should be passed to our Christ-loving and pious kings so that they can order the burning of the heretical books, full of evil doctrines and heresies, written by Theodoret. Let the inscribers go and read to Domnus, Archbishop of Antioch, what happened today, so he too can frankly comment on what he sees taking place.

As can be seen, Dioscorus did not render his judgment until the congregation was convinced of Theodoret's guilt.

19

As for Domnus, who did not attend this session, Dioscorus was keen to relay to him the minutes of the events and to have his comments. Therefore, it is surprising to note that such a great man (Dioscorus) is described as a violent, rapacious, unscrupulous, scandalously immoral man and an overbearing ecclesiastical dictator by the writers of the Roman Catholic Church, from whom most of the Western theological authors have gathered their information.[13] So far we are unable to find any real hard evidence pertaining to rapacity, immoral conduct, or dictatorship of Saint Dioscorus as claimed by Catholic historians. On the contrary:

> We find one thing clear which certainly tells in Dioscorus' favor. All the worst charges against him date from after the time when he [Dioscorus] was accused of heresy, and are much the same as those brought against Athanasius and other great men in like circumstances, which we dismiss as absolutely untrue. Dioscorus never had the same opportunity of publicly clearing himself from these imputations as Athanasius, but there is no good ground for supposing that he could not have done so. . . . John of Nikius and all other Egyptian historians speak of him with respect and affection. But more testimony in his favor is that of Theodoret of Cyrrhos, a man whom Dioscorus considered a heretic and who therefore cannot be accused of partiality to the Patriarch.[14]

In fact, the utmost testimony to the greatness of the Coptic Pope Dioscorus is that he preferred to go into exile and refused to acknowledge the decisions of the Council of Chalcedon. At the same council, he had the courage to excommunicate Leo of Rome after reading his tome in the Greek language.

Behavior of the others was less admirable:

1. Theodoret of Cyrrhos at Chalcedon anathematized his master Nestorius and, under pressure, denied what

20

he believed to be right and accepted the three letters of Cyril I.

2. Juvenal of Jerusalem crossed the floor of the house, joined the newly pardoned Nestorian group of Leo, and was allowed to retain the Patriarchal See of Jerusalem as a reward, an act that caused political upheaval among the Orthodox of the Church of Jerusalem.

The excommunication of Theodoret at Ephesus II passed without coercion and violence; otherwise, Theodoret would have mentioned it in his appeal to Leo (see appendix, p. 44) and would have certainly used it to strengthen his case against the proceedings of Ephesus II.

As we proceed to examine the case of Archbishop Domnus, we have to realize that at one stage, Dioscorus liked him. However, Domnus' weak personality was dominated by Theodoret of Cyrrhos. Therefore, it is not surprising to note that the See of Antioch was heavily populated by Nestorian bishops. Theodoret, unhampered by Domnus, preached Nestorian dogmas in the Churches of Antioch. This prompted Dioscorus to send two appeals to Domnus urging him to put an end to the heresies of Theodoret. (see appendix, p. 73.) According to the two letters, Dioscorus was appalled to see Nestorianism mushrooming not only in the Church of Antioch and the East at the hands of Theodoret of Cyrrhos, Ibas of Edessa, Basil of Seleucia, and other Eastern Bishops, but also gaining some ground in the land of Egypt. The letters exchanged between Rakotis and Antioch point clearly to the following:

1. Dioscorus firmly adhered to the canons of the two ecumenical councils held in Nicaea and Ephesus I. He correctly diagnosed the ailment of the Church in Antioch and moved swiftly and determinedly to eliminate

21

the source of trouble, as is obvious in his first letter to Domnus.

2. Again, Domnus was too weak to control the damaging activity of Theodoret and other Nestorianizers.

3. Understandably, and for nationalistic reasons, too, Domnus was faithful to the tradition of the school of Antioch and to the teachings of his predecessor John, as much as Dioscorus was to the school of Alexandria and to Athanasius and Cyril I of Rakotis.

4. No single word in the two letters of Dioscorus can be taken as evidence to support the Catholic historian's claim of an Apollinarian tendency in the school of Alexandria. On the contrary, Dioscorus confirmed that the human body of the Incarnate Word with a rational soul is consubstantial with ours, a profession of the true Orthodox faith versus the Nestorian heresy, which divides God into two separate natures after the incarnation. Dioscorus' orthodoxy was further confirmed in his two letters to his monks. (See appendix, pp. 75 and 76.)

Again, a sense of uneasiness and rage pervaded the council when the two letters of Dioscorus (Domnus' reply and a letter from Domnus to Flavian of Constantinople) were read to the bishops. The bishops considered the details of the letters as evidence of the involvement of Domnus with Nestorian and Theodorian heresies. Accordingly, they asked for his excommunication and condemnation. As documented in the minutes of Ephesus II, it was the bishop of Jerusalem and Cappadocia who presided over the lengthy deliberations examining the case of Domnus. In this instance, Dioscorus was considered a second party in the conflict, due to his exchange of letters with Domnus. Therefore, he did not participate in the proceedings.

Later Dioscorus informed the gathering: "The [members] of the great and holy council have heard what I have written to the pious Bishop Domnus, as it is my desire to keep peace in the Church. And as you can see, I did not go far beyond what my duties didacted. Very righteous [Fathers], please put it in writing if what I have written [to Domnus] negates the Orthodox belief."

The bishops of the council declared: "What you [Dioscorus] have proclaimed agrees with the faith of the Fathers. Yours is the credence of the Fathers, and conforms to the Orthodox beliefs. Yours concures with the canons of the Fathers of Nicaea; it agrees with the canons of the two councils [Nicaea and Ephesus I]. He who conceals these canons is not a good believer, he who does not confess this faith among people is not an honest believer, he who attacks these beliefs is not a true believer, and he who writes against it is not a fair believer."

In the end, the bishops condemned Domnus for supporting the dogmas of Nestorius and Theodoret. However, most surprising, is that Domnus was not reinstated at Chalcedon, while the two arch-Nestorianizers, Theodoret of Cyrrhos and Ibas of Edessa, were restored to office. Most likely, one can account for Domnus' unusual situation by considering two factors:

1. Domnus may have been a true Orthodox and the bishops of Ephesus II, including Dioscorus, utterly failed to comprehend the realities of the situation: Domnus was a weak prelate who was dominated by the strong orator Theodoret, i.e., he was unable to thwart or contain the activities of Theodoret.
2. At Chalcedon, Dioscorus was deposed, though not on doctrinal grounds, a move that was prearranged with Emperor Marcian and his wife, Pulcheria, for political

reasons. Naturally, the chief Nestorianizers (Theodoret, Ibas, Basil, Eusebius, and others) who catalyzed and paved the way for the downfall of Dioscorus were rewarded by being reinstated to their offices. Obviously, Domnus did not fit in and went unnoticed at Chalcedon.

Most probably the situation of Domnus was further complicated by his stand at Ephesus II regarding the case of Eutyches. After Juvenal of Jerusalem announced the orthodoxy of Eutyches [!], Domnus proclaimed: "I have earlier, according to the information received from the holy synod convened in the capital [Constantinople] with regard to the righteous archimandrite Eutyches, signed the documents of his deposition. But now that I am assured, based on the document he submitted, that he embraces the faith decreed by the three hundred and eighteen saintly Fathers, and the one hundred and fifty Bishops congregated in Ephesus, I too agree with Your Holiness that he [Eutyches] should be restored to the dignity of priesthood."

The bishops of Ephesus II also examined the case of Eutyches and Flavian. Even though the two cases are closely related, we will discuss them separately, for the sake of clarity.

The Case of Flavian

In brief, the assembly of bishops found Flavian guilty of harboring Nestorian dogmas and of sheltering Nestorianizers such as Basil of Seleucia and Eusebius of Dorylaeum. Accordingly, Flavian was excommunicated, and there is no reason whatsoever to entertain the idea that the bishops deposed Flavian against their consciences and will. However, the Catholic historians claim that the bishops at Ephesus II, who did not agree with Dioscorus, were terrorized by the monks of Barsumas and the royal guards and, in fear for their lives, they agreed to everything demanded of them, except for the Roman legates who managed to flee from the council [!].

Further, they claim that Flavian was kicked, knocked down, stabbed in the back, and trampled on and that the helpless patriarch died three days later of injuries he had received (!).[15] To optimize the case against Dioscorus, they claimed that Flavian, prior to his death, wrote an appeal to Leo with the help of one of the Roman legates, the deacon Hilarus. (See appendix, p. 47.) Several questions arise, such as:

1. How can a man who was kicked, knocked down, trampled on [!], and on the verge of death be able to formulate such an articulate appeal to Leo? Many authors expressed their doubts about the event.[16]
2. If Flavian was truly exposed to physical abuse, it would have been reasonable to think that Theodoret would have referred to this incident in his appeal to Leo to strengthen his case, especially since they were dealing with the same enemy, Dioscorus.
3. An accomplished Nestorian theologian such as Theodoret of Cyrrhos would have realized at once if there was any relationship between the Orthodox faith of Dioscorus and the heresies of Eutyches and would have definitely used it as a formidable weapon to counter the charges of Dioscorus and other bishops against him. Therefore, the claim of Flavian that the faith of Eutyches was preached and praised by Dioscorus is unfounded and leads us to doubt the Roman

25

legate's claim that Flavian was the author of the appeal to Leo.

4. If the Church and faith were deeply threatened by the decisions of Ephesus II, as it appears in Flavian's appeal, again, why did Theodoret not refer to it in his appeal? The rationale is straightforward: the decisions of Ephesus II are Orthodox and are in complete harmony with the canons of Nicaea and Ephesus I. What Theodoret was protesting was the injustice perpetrated against him in his absence at Ephesus II. However, it was Emperor Theodosius' order that confined Theodoret to his diocese, not that of Dioscorus.

5. How could Flavian claim that one sole man, Dioscorus, unsettled the faith established by the Fathers, showed his contempt to Leo's legate, caused riots, restored the condemned and condemned the innocents, and so on, in one day [!] unless the bishops of Ephesus II were very naive? Most of the bishops at Ephesus II were Orthodox Fathers, and it was natural to excommunicate the arch-Nestorians, without using the potential of physical coercion embodied in the royal guards.

Because of all the above factors, the argument that Flavian's appeal to Leo is a Roman synthesis is highly probable,[17] especially since Flavian was appealing to the Throne of the Apostolic See of Peter, the Prince of the Apostles, a notion that was initiated during the papacy of Leo.

The Case of Eutyches

Now, let us examine the case of Eutyches. At the beginning of this book, we illustrated how this cunning character deflected the questions of his inquisitors at the local council of Constantinople, A.D. 448, and how he was deliberately reluctant to concede that Christ's body is consubstantial with ours. Moreover, neither Flavian nor his bishops, Basil of Seleucia and Eusebius of Dorylaeum, were able to establish publicly Eutyches' fundamental heresies, which revolved about "commixtion and confusion" of the two natures in one after the Incarnation. There is no doubt that Eutyches was completely wrong, but his condemnation (by the bishops in Constantinople) appeared to be based on personal grudge rather than on doctrinal deviations, especially considering that the bishops refused to acknowledge Eutyches' written profession of faith, which was submitted to the council. They insisted on oral presentation and ensuing debate. Eutyches knew how to exploit the situation diplomatically by replying in vaguely worded statements.

At Ephesus II, Eutyches presented a long written statement on faith, which was taken as evidence of his beliefs. As we review the documents of Eutyches (see appendix, p. 50), we recognize several important points, namely:

1. Eutyches confirmed that he adhered to the creed of Nicaea, according to which he was living, baptized in it after he had received it from his parents [!]. Furthermore, he wished to die in this belief and that of Ephesus I as articulated by Cyril I of happy memory [!].

2. Eutyches anathematized Mani, Apollinarius, Nestorius, and other heretics, even Simon the Witch, who claimed that the body of our Lord and God had descended from Heaven [!]. In this context, we may also note that Eutyches avoided any reference to what he

27

truly believed to be the nature of the body of Christ, which was the focus of his heresy. Thus Eutyches managed to leave a strong impression of his orthodoxy on the minds of the bishops.

3. Eutyches clearly refuted the accusation of Flavian by stating that "while I was serenely living in the faith of Nicaea and Ephesus I, Eusebius of Dorylaeum directed the accusation against me as he placed a complaint to the righteous Bishop Flavian and other bishops who were then at the capital for different purposes. He [Eusebius] called me a blasphemer to humiliate me and did not include one point of the so-called heresy in his document." Eutyches also documented that he had refused to yield to the pressure, applied on him by the bishops congregated at the synod of Constantinople, to renounce the faith of the Fathers of Nicaea and Ephesus I.

4. Again, Eutyches knew how to emote the compassion of the bishops, for example, by his assertion that his condemnation was prepared in advance as if by a settled agreement. He also documented that:

the righteous Bishop Flavian did not utter one single good word in my favor, which compelled me to seek the help of your Holiness. He, Flavian, was not even embarrassed by my advanced age, I who spent my life struggling against the heretics, fighting for the orthodox faith [!]. And as if he [Flavian] solely had the power to decide everything that pertained to the faith, nor did he recognize one's right to stand up for his rights; he passed his judgment against me, excommunicated me from the Church as he claimed, stripped me of priesthood as he thought, prevented me from presiding over the cloister, and handed me over to the mobs who had been placed in the bishopric and the streets, for the purpose of attacking me as a heretic, a blasphemer and a Mani. And if I had not been saved and

28

protected by Divine Providence till this day, to have your Holiness pity me, I would have perished.

Based on the above, the bishops, including Domnus, Basil of Seleucia, and others who had previously condemned Eutyches at the synod of Constantinople, declared Eutyches an Orthodox [!] in response to Dioscorus' request: "Now that everything has been understood, let the pious convened bishops, one by one, declare what he understood about the faith of the archimandrite Eutyches and what is his judgment." The prelates, speaking one after another, declared in Eutyches' favor, and he was reinstated by Juvenal of Jerusalem and the bishop of Cappadocia.

Again, we cannot find any evidence to support the claim that the bishops acquitted Eutyches against their will. However, Flavian, in the so-called appeal to Leo, complained that he was not allowed to defend his actions against Eutyches in Constantinople: "Dioscorus gave order that I and the bishops who sat in judgment with me, and my clergy also, should not be allowed any hearing or the utterance of a word of defence on any point. . . . This is, of course, erroneous; Emperor Theodosius stated clearly in his letter to the imperial commissioner:

We are confident that you would not allow any violence to be instigated by the two parties [Flavian and Eutyches]. If you have found someone who tries to agitate violence, thus negating the holy faith, treat him with caution and keep us informed; and let all proceedings go according to order, because you [will] be in the court of deliberations. Make every effort that the subjects should be examined carefully and as quickly as possible by the holy council, and keep us informed. Since those who excommunicated the righteous archimandrite Eutyches will be attending, they should be silent, as the arrangement of the council dictates that they should not speak but wait for collective agreement which will take place between other Holy Fathers, because the issues for which he [Eutyches] was judged are currently under examination, for no one, whoever that may be, is allowed to intervene before the confirmation of the Orthodox faith is affirmed. . . .

That the "wicked old" Eutyches returned to his heretic dogmas after being reinstated by the Ephesian II Council does not justify staining Dioscorus and the Fathers of Ephesus II as "Monophysite heretics" and labeling the council as a "den of robbers." These unfortunate accusations, made by Leo, reflected his state of mind at the time. He, who regarded himself as the supreme Pope, was enraged that his tome was neither read nor accepted by the Fathers of Ephesus II. Further, Flavian, a man whom Leo supported, was condemned and excommunicated together with other Nestorian bishops. Leo was also aggravated by the fact that his attempts to influence the decisions of Ephesus II, even before the bishops initiated their deliberations, were in vain, especially since his legates were hardly able to follow the course of arguments completely as it was conducted in Greek.

In this context, we should not be particularly severe in our criticism of Leo. While the East (Rakotis and Antioch) produced great Christian thinkers, the Latin West (Rome) was still in its theological infancy. At any rate, the decisions of Ephesus II secured Leo's lasting hostility for Dioscorus. Leo pursued every avenue to crush him. He wrote to prominent religious and political figures, including the Emperor of the West, Valentinian, Pulcheria, and others, stressing the necessity of a general council to reserve the decisions of Ephesus II in order to rescue the Christian faith [!]. Such an opportunity came to Leo when Theodosius fell off his horse and died (July, A.D. 450). His sister Pulcheria, a nun and married to one of her soldiers, called Marcian, under the auspices of Leo, was now in control of the empire. Marcian, as a professional soldier, realized that the powerful Popes of Rakotis had consolidated the Egyptian nation under the name of the Church.[18]

The growing power of the Egyptian Pope, Dioscorus, and the fear of losing the wheat from the most fertile Oriental province in the Eastern Empire were the immediate danger to the Byzantine Empire. Out of the political fear of Marcian and his wife and Leo's hatred to Dioscorus, a new alliance was born. Surely, the accusation of heresy was the formidable weapon against the ascendancy of Dioscorus. Egypt, at the height of its spiritual dominance, had the seeds of its own destruction germinating in its soils watered generously by the hands of her very beloved sons. Anatolius, who was Dioscorus' commissary at Constantinople and was consecrated as patriarch, betrayed his master in order to appease Marcian and his wife and to secure Leo's agreement to the claim of Constantinople as the second see of Christendom.[19]

The Council of Chalcedon

As is clear from the correspondence between Marcian and Leo, the condemnation of Dioscorus was already agreed upon. Leo then wrote to the Fathers of Ephesus II to sway their thoughts, and, in his later correspondence with Marcian, he suggested that the issue was not the "heresy of Eutyches" or the "tyrannic conduct of Dioscorus," because these matters had been settled already [!], but the issue was on what basis clemency should be bestowed to those bishops who participated in Ephesus II (whom, he claimed, were influenced by Dioscorus' threats of violence). In the final analysis, Leo was a great politician, but certainly was neither a great theologian nor an impartial prelate.

Many of the Church historians have ignored, for various reasons, the following valuable piece of information. Initially, Marcian issued a summon for a council to be held at Constantinople. Dioscorus attended and was surprised to see many of the excommunicated Nestorianizers among the bishops. After the Tome of Leo was read in the meeting, Saint Dioscorus accused him openly of Nestorianizing the Orthodox faith and went into depth explaining the faith of Nicaea and Ephesus I. The words of Dioscorus were clearcut: "We believe that our Lord Jesus Christ is perfect God with respect to His Divinity and is perfect man with respect to His humanity. In Him, His Divinity is united with His humanity in a real perfect union without mingling, without commixtion, without confusion, without alteration, without division and without separation. His Divinity did not separate from His humanity for an instant. In Him are preserved all the properties of Divinity and all the properties of humanity, together in a real, perfect, indivisible and inseparable union." The bishops, hearing the strong words of Dioscorus, shouted, "We are all in the same belief!" Emperor Marcian, who was attending the meeting, suggested to the legates of Leo that they postpone the meeting.[20] It seems that the emperor was still hopeful for a peaceful conclusion in Leo's favor. Therefore, he invited some bishops and Dioscorus to a special meeting in the imperial palace. They proposed to Dioscorus that he yield to the emperor so that he would retain his patriarchal see. Dioscorus replied: "The Emperor does not need to indulge into these delicate issues, but should order and look after the matters of his Empire and let the clergy decide on the Orthodox faith because they know the books, and he should not be biased and should

32

follow the truth." Most surprisingly, Pulcheria also participated in the religious conflict. She reminded Dioscorus of the fate of John Chrysostom, patriarch of Constantinople from A.D. 389 to 404: "Dioscorus! in the time of my mother [Eudoxia] there was a stubborn man [John Chrysostom] like you. He was excommunicated and dethroned." Obviously, Dioscorus understood her meaning. The great Copt did not bend and replied, "You know what happened to your mother and how she caught the disease that you know about. It was not until she went to the relics of John Chrysostom and asked for forgiveness that she was healed."

When Marcian realized that Dioscorus was not going to submit, he gave his orders. Dioscorus was savagely beaten by the guards; they pulled out the hair of his beard and broke some of his teeth. Dioscorus sent his torn hair and broken teeth to Egypt with the very short historic appellation to the Copts: "This is the fruit of protecting the faith."

The Bishops moved to Chalcedon to commence their meeting together with Dioscorus and his Coptic bishops. On October 8, 451, the Church of Saint Euphemia witnessed the council's opening. As expected, Theodoret, bishop of Cyrrhos, arrived to the shouts and protests of council members, and, as a result, most bishops lost their self-control and exchanged bitter accusations. The council almost broke into riot and violence. Dioscorus behaved with great self-command and dignity, refraining from participating in the unfortunate upheaval.

Dioscorus sat in judgment, and Eusebius of Dorylaeum opened the case for the prosecution. Needless to say, Leo and Marcian restored the Nestorianizers to their previous positions in the religious hierarchy to use them against Dioscorus. The Roman legates accused Dioscorus of holding a general council without prior approval from Rome and demanded his withdrawal from the congregation. The imperial commissioners ignored their request, because there was no such precedent for securing the permission of Rome prior to holding a general council. Nevertheless, Dioscorus replied that Emperor Theodosius requested that Ephesus II be held, and consequently, Dioscorus asked that its acts be read. His request was approved. However, harsh shouts and outcries from both sides interrupted the readings. Once again, Dioscorus showed great reserve by refusing to join the partisan debate. While the acts were being read by the inscribers, many bishops denied their former declarations made at Ephesus II, when they realized that they did not coincide with the thoughts expressed at Chalcedon. It seems that the acts were read from the copy of Dioscorus, because these bishops kept on challenging it. Dioscorus shrewdly pointed out that the inscribers of the bishops of Jerusalem and Cappadocia and many others were similarly documenting the minutes of Ephesus II and asked to have the acts read from their copies. Although the different set of acts matched, these bishops insisted on denying their former proclamations and Dioscorus exclaimed, "If they deny all these known proclamations, why did not they then claim we were not attending?!"

The council then moved to discuss the case of Flavian. Once Dioscorus' judgment on Flavian and Eusebius of Dorylaeum at Ephesus II was read, the pardoned Nestorians shouted, "Anathema to Dioscorus! This hour condemns him; this hour he is damned. Blessed Lord, avenge him [Flavian]: holy Emperor, avenge him. Long live Leo! Long live the patriarch." Again, shouts and cries broke out in the council. However, the imperial commissioners were able to restore peace to the council, which allowed Dioscorus to give his rational in the excommunication of

34

Flavian: "The reason why Flavian was condemned was plainly this: that he confessed of two natures after the Incarnation. I have passages from the Fathers Athanasius, Gregory and Cyril to the effect that after the Incarnation there were not two natures, but one Incarnate nature of the Word. If I am to be condemned, the Fathers will be condemned with me. I am defending their doctrine. I do not deviate from them at all. I have not acquired these documents carelessly. I have verified them." Further, Dioscorus gave a careful statement of faith disclaiming all notions of confusion, commixtion, mixture, and mingling of the Divine Nature and the Human Nature of Christ after the Incarnation.

Basil of Seleucia, when asked by the commissioners, declared that he subscribed to Flavian's condemnation because "I had to agree with the one hundred and twenty or one hundred and thirty bishops who approved his excommunication."

Dioscorus confidently questioned him: "You feared declaring your faith to people to flatter them. Thus, you betrayed virtue and insulted the faith. Do you not know there is no hypocrisy in faith?"

However, when the bishops of the East supported Basil's claim that they too subscribed, under pressure and threats from the commissioners of Emperor Theodosius, to the condemnation of Flavian, the Coptic bishops rebuked them: "The Christian is fearless; the Orthodox does not quiver; set us on fire and we will show you how martyrs die."

Dioscorus added, "That they claim they were forced to sign a blank paper which [their conduct] in itself betrays their episcopal duties; the issue relates to the grace of faith, and the grace of faith necessitates courage associated with knowledge."

The words of Dioscorus and his Coptic bishops went

35

to no avail, simply because his fate had already been concluded. Falsified evidence as to the tyranny and violence of Dioscorus at Ephesus II was submitted.

At Chalcedon, the Roman legates propagated the Tome of Leo and their Nestorianizing friends approved it. Many others, notably Bishop Atticus of Nicopolis, found that the emphasis on the two natures of Christ in Leo's Tome was too much to accept[21] and requested additional time to study it. This was approved, and the commissioners appointed the council to meet again in five days. In this context, Dioscorus noticed the fingerprints of Theodoret of Cyrrhos when he read the Greek version of the Tome of Leo and refused to subscribe to it in one of those decisive statements of his. The great Coptic national said, " . . . and even if they severed my hand, with its blood pouring on this document [Leo's Tome], I am not subscribing to it." Dioscorus coupled his strong words with strong actions; in the midst of hostile Nestorianizers and potential enemies, he confirmed the excommunication of both Theodoret and Leo.

Three days later, the council convened under pressure from the Roman legates. Even though Dioscorus was officially notified three times, he was unable to attend the meeting because the Roman legates gave strict orders to the imperial guards to confine Dioscorus to his cell. In reality, Dioscorus was under house arrest, and the plot against him reached its final stages. The Roman legates, Marcian, and his Nestorianizer friends knew that it would be rather impossible to condemn Dioscorus on theological grounds and that his very presence in the council would be fatal to their cause. Therefore, they arranged for his excommunication on technical grounds, i.e., failure to attend a general council after the third official notification. In the absence of Dioscorus, numerous reckless accusations, brought against him by the rehabilitated Nestorians, were readily accepted by the Roman legates. We have to remember that similar charges were brought by the Arians against his predecessor, Athanasius of Rakotis.

Dioscorus was deposed and exiled to Gangra, where he lived quietly and passed away five years later. During these bleak years, Dioscorus behaved with a dignity worthy of a great Coptic sovereign who occupies the throne of Saint Mark.

In their hour of triumph, Marcian and Leo did not comprehend the blunder they committed against the empire and the Church respectively. The consequences were grave indeed.

The East was dispirited. It refused to recognize the authority of the Chalcedonian bishop appointed by the imperial court and consecrated its own Orthodox bishops. Frequent revolts erupted and were put down most violently, especially in Egypt, by the imperial guards. Naturally, the southern part of the Byzantine Empire was weakened, and it was not until A.D. 640 that the barefoot Arab soldiers under the slogan of the new religion, Islam, conquered Egypt, the fertile province that Marcian and Leo cared about very much. It was not only Egypt, but also Syria, Palestine, and the Penta Polis that fell into the hands of the Arabs.

As for Leo, Rome became the supreme See of the empire, as he had always wished, but he managed to split the Church for the first time in history.

Marcian despatched four bishops to Rakotis to supervise the election of a new archbishop. The betrayal was from within; Proterius, the archpriest from Alexandria who was appointed by Dioscorus to look after the affairs of the Church in his absence, was assigned the post after he accepted the decisions of the Council of Chalcedon and the Tome of Leo. Fourteen bishops out of the hundred Coptic bishops supported and cooperated with Proterius. The Copts rejected the decrees of Chalcedon, and Proterius was labeled "the traitor" and "the emperor's bishop." The rage and fury of the Copts over the deposition of Dioscorus knew no limits. For them, Dioscorus was the Pope as long as he lived, the leader and the symbol of true Christian Orthodoxy. The Copts burst into anger the very same night of Proterius' consecration; riots broke out in every corner of the city. The soldiers were called to quench the uprise. At the end of the evening, the blood of the Copts stained most of the streets of Rakotis.

Proterius, who extorted the throne of Saint Dioscorus, was like the Arians who had been intruded in place of Saint Athanasius.

In 454, Pope Dioscorus passed away, but the Egyptians were unable to choose a new Pope before the death of Emperor Marcian in 457. A pious monk from the monastry of Kalamoun was selected and consecrated by the bishops as Timothy, Pope of Rakotis. Proterius, who symbolized the Byzantine oppressor, robbed the Coptic churches and amassed the treasures in his residence. Upon the emperor's death in 457, the Copts demonstrated against the emperor's bishop and the country was again in turmoil. Thieves seized this opportunity to kill Proterius and loot his residency.

Archbishop Leo of Rome regretted his rigidity and in 458, in a letter to the Egyptians, he formulated his understanding on the Incarnation in Cyrillian terms, but it was too late. The schism between Alexandria and Rome was sealed with the death of Saint Dioscorus.

In brief, the 170 years that followed the Council of Chalcedon were years of violence. All types of pressure were applied on the Coptic Church by the Byzantine court to bring the Church to its knees. During this period of time, the Church of Saint Mark witnessed the Chalcedonian bishops imposed by the imperial court, but the chain of the Orthodox Coptic patriots elected to the throne of Saint Mark was never interrupted until today. These long years of struggle annihilated the strength of the Coptic people and the Church. The Copts could not temper the feeling of bitterness and disillusion they harbored concerning the Christian oppressors.

In A.D. 640, the night came after a long day and Egypt's soul was engulfed in darkness from which she never woke up. One tyranny replaced another.

APPENDIX

The Letter of Leo to Eutyches

To the beloved son [child] Eutyches the priest and archimandrite, from Bishop Leo,

It came to our knowledge from your appeal [letter] that some with perverted tendencies have recently renewed the dogma of Nestorius. And we were pleased that you opposed them. We have no doubt at all that the Lord Who gave us the same belief would support your efforts. As for us, and after we have known of the hypocrisy of those supporting Nestorius, we see that our duty is to destroy the evil, and may the Almighty God protect you.

The Letter of the Emperors of the East and West to Dioscorus

From the Emperors Caesar Theodosius and Valentinian, the conquerors, to Dioscorus, Patriarch of Rakotis,

Since it became known that our general mission and endeavors are supported and upheld in the fear of the Lord, and if the Lord supports what we are aiming for, our deeds will attain the highest ends. And we called for preaching what pertains to God's will in order to make every effort to establish peace and tranquility among our subjects, so that our true faith would be supported in the absolute fear of God. And now disputes arose and are about to distort the Apostolic teachings and Orthodox faith. If conflicting thoughts were attractive to humans, they would corrupt people's consciences and bewilder their souls. We have not thought it right to allow such evils with these characteristics to spread; otherwise our carelessness would cause injustice to the Lord. For these reasons, we have decreed the God-loving bishops, who are distinguished by absolute piety and with the true Orthodox faith, to convene to investigate the matters carefully so that the true Orthodox faith, which satisfies God, prevails. Accordingly, we ask Your Holiness to come to Ephesus without delay, accompanied by ten archbishops from your jurisdiction and ten bishops who are known for their ability, excellence, knowledge, erudition, and true Orthodox faith. The uninvited should not attend the council, in order not to unsettle it. Only the bishops to whom we sent this letter and who are invited to this city should come with great interest to investigate the matters precisely to uproot the evil from its source and let the true Orthodox faith, which satisfies our Savior Christ, illuminate the faith to which people should adhere to now and in the future without deviation, through the support of the Almighty God.

Our orders should be obeyed by those who exalted themselves from deviance, with all their faculties, to come to the designated place. Those who absent themselves without a major reason will be guilty of conscience and will not find pardon before God and us.

As for Theodoret Bishop of Cyrrhos, he has to remain in his Church as we ordered him earlier and is prohibited from attending this holy council, unless the convened bishops themselves may decide otherwise for conversance, and if conflict arises because of him, the council shall judge.

This is our decree and order.[22]

The Imperial Order Read to the Bishops at the Opening of the Council of Ephesus II

From Emperors Caesar Theodosius and Valentinian, the conquerors, to the Council of Ephesus,

We hoped that God's Holy Church would be without any problem while you were performing your usual liturgical services, without causing you that much trouble [of traveling to Ephesus]. However, the God-loving Bishop Flavian has summoned a council [Constantinople] and inquired into the laws of faith against the archimandrite Eutyches. We have asked this God-loving bishop several times to eliminate such discord, because we trust that the faith we received from the holy Fathers [congregated] in Nicaea and Ephesus is complete. On several occasions, we have asked this pious bishop to evade raising this subject, thereby averting a widespread strife. However, he did not yield. Therefore, we found it imperative to call for a holy council to investigate tenets of our faith in a group of pious and holy bishops. The timely issues are to be laid out and examined with the intention of eradicating evil at its inception and removing from the Holy Church all those who adhere to the heresies of Nestorius or support him and decreeing the support of the Orthodox faith, firmly and without reluctance. All our hope and the strength of our empire depend on firm belief in the Lord and your holy prayers.

Pope Dioscorus Presides over Ephesus II

From Emperors Caesar Theodosius and Valentinian, the conquerors, to Dioscorus, patriarch of Rakotis:

We have decreed earlier that Theodoret, bishop of Cyrrhos, was not to attend the holy council. This is until the holy council decides on what is suitable with regard to him. We have overlooked him because he dared and wrote against the laws of faith decreed by Cyril of holy memory, bishop of the great [city] Rakotis. Those who adopted the dogmas of Nestorius may try laboriously to introduce him [Theodoret] to the holy council. Therefore, we found it necessary to draw the attention to that [issue] in our imperial writings, directing our letter to you, O God-loving, and to the holy council. As we are adhering to the laws of the Saintly Fathers, not only with regard to Theodoret but also with regard to all who are worthy of attending the council now we assign you, O God-loving, the primacy and authority over the council and confirm God-loving Archbishop Juvenal of Jerusalem and God-loving Archbishop Thalassius to be with you. And let these, virtuous, conscience, loving, and supporting the Orthodox faith, be your counselors. Those who omitted or added to the canons of faith decreed in Nicaea and later confirmed by the Council of Ephesus, we order that they should not have a say in the congregation, and wish that their fate is dependent on your judgment. Therefore, we ask the holy council to convene now.

The Appeal of Theodoret to Leo

For the very righteous bishop of Alexandria was not content with the illegal and very unrighteous deposition of the most holy and godly bishop of Constantinople, the lord Flavian, nor was his soul satisfied with a similar slaughter of the rest of the bishops, but me, too, in my absence he stabbed with a pen, without summoning me to trial, without trying me in my presence, without questioning me as to my opinions about the Incarnation of our God and Savior. Even murderers, tomb-breakers, and adulterers are not condemned by their judges until either they have themselves confirmed by confession the charges brought against them or have been clearly convicted by the testimony of others. Yet I, nurtured as I have been in the divine laws, have been condemned by him at his pleasure, when all the while I was five and thirty days' march away.

Nor is this all that he has done. Only last year when two fellows tainted with the unsoundness of Apollinarius had gone thither and patched up slanders against me, he stood up in church and anathematized me and that after I had written to him and explained my opinions to him.

I lament the storm raging over the Church and long for peace. Six and twenty years have I ruled the Church entrusted to me by the God of all, aided by your prayers. Never in the time of the blessed Theodotus, the chief bishop of the East, never in the time of his successors in the see of Antioch, did I incur the slightest blame. By the help of God's grace working with me, I rescued more than a thousand souls from the plague of Marcion; many others from the Arian and Eunomian factions did I bring over to our Master Christ. I have done pastoral duty in eight hundred churches, for so many parishes does Cyrrhos contain; and in them, through your prayers, not even one tare is left, and our flock is delivered from all heresy and error. He who sees all things knows how many stones have been cast at me by heretics of ill repute, how many conflicts in most of the cities of the East I have waged against paganism, against Jews, against every heretical

45

error. After all this sweat and toil I have been condemned without a trial.

But I await the sentence of your Apostolic See. I beseech and implore Your Holiness to succour me in my appeal to your fair and righteous tribunal. Bid me hasten to you and prove to you that my teaching follows the footprints of the apostles. I have in my possession what I wrote twenty years ago, what I wrote eighteen, fifteen, twelve years ago, against Arians and Eunomians, against Jews and pagans; against the magi in Persia, on universal providence, on theology, and on the Divine Incarnation. By God's grace I have interpreted the writings of the apostles and the oracles of the prophets. From these it is not difficult to ascertain whether I have adhered to the right rule of faith or have swerved from its straight course. Do not, I implore you, spurn my prayer; regard, I implore you, the insults piled after all my labors on my poor grey head.

Above all, I implore you to tell me whether I ought to put up with this unrighteous deposition or not, for I await your decision. If you bid me abide by the sentence of condemnation, I abide, and henceforth I will trouble no man and will wait for the unbiased tribunal of our God and Savior. God is my witness that I care not for honor and glory. I care only for the scandal that has been caused, in that many of the simpler folk, and especially those whom I have rescued from various heresies, cleaving to the authority of my judges and quite unable to understand the exact truth of the doctrine, will perhaps suppose me guilty of heresy.

All the people of the East know that during all the time of my episcopate I have not acquired a house, not a piece of ground, not a farthing, not a tomb, but of my own accord have embraced poverty, after distributing, at the

46

death of my parents, the whole of the property that I inherited from them.

Flavian's Appeal to Leo

To the most religious and blessed Father and Archbishop Leo, Flavian sends greeting in the Lord.

I had good cause for referring my present situation to Your Holiness and for using an appeal to your apostolic authority, asking that it should reach out to the East and bring help to the pious faith of the Holy Fathers, which they have handed down to us with such toil and sweat, and which is now in danger. Everything is in complete confusion; the laws of the Church are abolished; in matters of faith all is lost; pious souls are bewildered by controversy. Men do not now speak of the faith of the Fathers, but the fact is that the views of Eutyches are now preached and praised by Dioscorus, bishop of Alexandria, and those who think as he does. For his decree is the confirmation of this "faith," as is the vote of those bishops who had been compelled by force to agree to it. I find it impossible to refer to your blessedness each several circumstance, but we shall explain briefly to you what happened.

[The bishops had arrived at Ephesus, in accordance with the imperial summons, and met Leo's legates. There was general agreement among the bishops, except for the Alexandrian contingent, whose previous contempt for the writer had been very marked.

Dioscorus suddenly called the council together; he refused any general consideration of the decisions of Nicaea or of Ephesus (431)] but, giving orders that I and the bishops who sat in judgment with me, and my clergy also, should not be allowed any hearing or the utterance of a

47

word of defence on any point, threatening also some with various punishments, he clears the way for the immediate reading in our presence of an account of the matter previously prepared by Eutyches.

After this, he directed the aforesaid Eutyches to put in a written charge against me, and when this was read, treating me as unworthy of any argument or question, he rose at once to his feet, declared him Catholic, reinstating him in the priesthood, and also compelled some bishops against their will to make the same declaration.

Shortly afterwards he proposed the reading of the canons formerly enacted at Ephesus, in which is contained the decree that "if anyone attempt to disturb the settlement there made by the Fathers, being a bishop, he shall be deposed" and so on. That sentence should be effective against Eutyches, who so openly declared himself for the introduction of Apollinarianism. Yet Dioscorus did nothing of the kind, but proposed the condemnation of me and Eusebius, the bishops all weeping, and would not grant to their entreaties a postponement for a single day; and having made this motion, he compelled some of the other bishops to assent to this abominable condemnation, swords being drawn upon those who wished for a postponement on the ground that he would not allow the letter of Your Holiness to be read, since that would sufficiently establish the faith of our fathers, but neglecting what might open the way of truth even to angry and brutal minds, and requiring statements irrational and full of blindness to be received and read, he treated your delegates as if they were unworthy to utter a single word, but with a sort of rush shamefully managed by him alone, all wrongs, so to say, were suddenly packed into one day, riots, the restoration of the condemned, the condemnation of the innocent, of men who have never in any way thought of transgressing against the authority of the Fathers. And since all was going unjustly against me, as if by a settled agreement, after the iniquitous proposal, which, of his own motion he levelled at me, on my appealing to the throne of the Apostolic See of Peter, the Prince of the Apostles, and to the holy council in general which meets under Your Holiness a crowd of soldiers at once surrounds me, prevents me from taking refuge at the holy altar, as I desired, and tried to drag me out of the church. Then, amid the utmost tumult, I barely succeeded in reaching a certain part of the church, and there I hid myself with my companions, not without being watched, however, to prevent my reporting to you all the wrongs that have been done me.

I therefore beseech Your Holiness not to let things rest in regard to this mad plot that has been carried out against me, since there are no grounds for bringing me into judgment; but rise up first in the cause of our right faith, which has been recklessly destroyed, and further, in view of the violated laws of the Church, assume their guardianship, simply stating the facts throughout to the more honorable among the people, and instructing with suitable letters our faithful and Christian emperor.

Theodoret Complains to Dioscorus of Alexandria

Thus I was compelled to write when I read the letters of Your Holiness to the most pious and sacred Archbishop Domnus, for there was contained in them the statement that certain men have come to the illustrious city administered by Your Holiness and have accused me of dividing the one Lord Jesus Christ into two sons, and this when preaching at Antioch, where innumerable hearers swell the congregation. I wept for the men who had the hardihood to contrive the vain calumny against me. But I grieved, and, my Lord, forgive me, forced as I am by pain to speak, that Your Pious Excellency did not reserve one ear unbiased for me instead of believing the lies of my accusers. Yet they were but three or four or about a dozen while I have countless hearers to testify to the orthodoxy of my teaching. Six years I continued teaching in the time of Theodotus, bishop of Antioch, of blessed and sacred memory, who was famous alike for his distinguished career and for his knowledge of the divine doctrines. Thirteen years I taught in the time of Bishop John of sacred and blessed memory, who was so delighted at my discourses as to raise both his hands and again and again to start up; Your Holiness, in your own letters has borne witness how, brought up as he was from boyhood with the divine oracles, the knowledge which he had of the divine doctrines was most exact. Besides these, this is the seventh year of the Most Pious Lord Archbishop Domnus. Up to this present day, after the lapse of so long a time, not one of the pious bishops, not one of the devout clergy, has ever at any time found any fault with my utterances. And with how much gratification Christian people hear our discourses, your godly Excellency can easily learn from travelers in one direction and another.

The Letter of Eutyches to the Bishops of Ephesus II

To the holy ecumenical council in the cathedral of the city of Ephesus, from Eutyches the archimandrite:

I thank the Holy God this day in which for your sake, God, fear was exalted. I advise your holy council of what befell me, that which occurred against the Orthodox faith. for I have decided since childhood to retreat into seclusion with myself until agedness so as I can be far away from every agitation. However, I was not left to enjoy the beatitude of sweet contemplation; thus my inner peace was disturbed by the advancing danger from others.

I, according to the definitions of your first holy council assembled here, have not conformed except to the faith decreed by the holy Fathers in the city of Nicaea, and before explaining what befell me, I clearly proclaim the holy faith that I hold for the relief of your conscience, you holy men, as God and Your Holiness are my witness. I, with all my strength, fought the heretics, always supporting the Orthodox faith. I believe in one God, the Father, the Almighty, Maker of heaven and earth, of all that is seen and unseen. I believe in one Lord Jesus Christ, the only Son of God, eternally begotten of the Father, God from God, Light from Light, True God from True God, begotten not made, of one Being with the Father. Through Him all things were made. For us men and for our salvation He came down from heaven by the power of the Holy Spirit. He became Incarnate from the Virgin Mary and was made man. For our sake He was crucified under Pontius Pilate; He suffered death and was buried. On the third day He rose again in accordance with the Scriptures; He ascended into heaven and is seated at the right hand of the Father. He will come again in glory to judge the living and the dead, and His kingdom will have no end.

As it were, I have embraced the faith from my parents. In it I was born and consecrated myself to God, whose mercy accepted me; with this belief I was anointed in baptism. So I lived in it to this day, and I pray to cease in it. For that creed was supported, as I have mentioned, by the holy ecumenical council congregated here, which was chaired by his beatitude our father Bishop Cyril of happy memory. It was ordained he who reissues what has been decreed or believes or preaches against it makes himself liable to certain punishments versed out in that decree. It is the faith, I relate to the writings of our father Cyril who was numbered with the Saints, it is the faith which my hands embrace and according to it I submit to the holy council and am bound to its dictums to this moment. And I do consider all the holy Orthodox Saintly Fathers, as you, most pious believers and chose them as masters for me.

I condemn Mani, Valentinian, Apollinarius, Nestorius, and all the heretics, even Simon the Witch, and those who claimed that the body of our Lord descended from heaven.

While I was in this faith, serenely living and praying, Eusebius, bishop of Dorylaeum, directed the accusation against me as he placed a complaint to the righteous Bishop Flavian and other bishops who were at the capital for different purposes. He [Eusebius] called me a blasphemer to humiliate me, and did not include one point of the so-called heresy in his document. This was to surprise me while being interrogated, stun me that words would fail me, and in the assembled synod [Eusebius] agitated enormous enigma and challenged me with the document of condemnation, and beside him was another avenger [Flavian] who was neither tender at heart nor merciful. He thought I would not come because I was restored to seclusion in the monastery, therefore, the righteous bishop decreed my excommunication in advance, as he thought I was not attending. I was assured of that from the honorable patrician who was appointed by our God-loving king to protect me from the danger that threatened my life. I knew that when I came from the cloister to the capital, where I was assured by the honorable patrician

52

that my attendance was to no avail, because the edict of my deposition was already prepared before investigation. This became clear to me later. However, I attended the synod to defend my dogma.

I have submitted a written document of faith and signed it as it was faith that was decreed by the Saintly Fathers in Nicaea and approved by the holy council of Ephesus I. However, it was refused and was not read. Tumult and mixed confusion broke out in the synod, and many aggressively encircled me and were screaming in unusual voices, yearning to coerce me to answer impetuously. It can be concluded from the arbitration documented in the minutes how the bishops bore me a grudge. I was ordered to give verbally the formula of my faith, and said that I maintain the faith of the saintly three hundred and eighteen Fathers who met in Nicaea and confirmed by the holy council of Ephesus. I was requested to proclaim a different faith to that decreed in Nicaea and Ephesus. As for me, I feared breaching the ordinance that was decreed in the holy council convened here earlier and that was canonized by the Saintly Fathers congregated in Nicaea concerning faith. However, I wish it will become known to your holy council that I am agreeable to what Your Holiness will decide upon.

While I was progressing in declaring the faith, I was astounded by the decree of deposition that was prepared earlier against me. The decree was read in the same spirit, and the exchange of words between me and them was documented in the minutes. This was followed by many accusations, especially while I was proclaiming my confession according to the decree of our Saintly Fathers of Nicaea and the Fathers who convened later in Ephesus. And everything was distorted before its registration: and distortion applies to the rest of the decisions. Howbeit my petition and the order of our Christ-loving and believing king, the righteous Bishop Flavian did not utter one single good word in my favor, which compelled me to seek the help of Your Holiness. He was not even embarrassed by my advanced age, I who spent my life struggling against the heretics, fighting for the Orthodox faith. And as if he [Flavian] solely had the power to decide everything that pertained to faith, nor did he recognize one's right to stand up for his rights; he passed his judgment against me, excommunicated me from the Church as he claimed, stripped me of priesthood, as he thought, prevented me from participating in the rituals of the holy sacrament, unfairly deposed me from presiding over the cloister, and handed me over to the mobs, who had been placed in the bishopric for the purpose of attacking me as a heretic, blasphemer, and Mani. And if I were not saved and protected by the Divine Providence till this day, to have Your Holiness pity me, I would have perished.

He declared the judgment against me, and it was read in various gatherings and saints' commemorations immediately, and condemned with me all those who may contact me or talk to me, and estranged me from communion with God. He did not hesitate to force the archimandrites to sign to the judgment decreed against me, not waiting for your holy council. There is no law that permits this, even against the heretics, as you, God-loving, know. He even sent these decisions to the East and other countries and unfairly forced many of the bishops and pious monks to subscribe to it without hearings. It was the duty, first and above all, that he should have written to the bishops about these incidents that I have mentioned. I was hardly saved and registered it [the incidents] in this document to be known to everyone, and I submit it to the Lord's love dwelling in you. I have asked the believer and pious emperor that you, pure and pious, be the judge of my case, you who despise unfairness and coercion.

I ask now, Your Holiness, to imagine that unfairness and damage done to me and the consequent calamity in the holy Church of God everywhere and the doubts of many as a result of it. With your Christ-loving wisdom, impose Church punishment on those who caused this [turmoil], thus eradicating heresy and hypocrisy from its origin. As for me, I have succumbed from the very beginning to the judgment of your beatitudes, and I confess the Orthodox faith to Jesus Christ, who confessed in the presence of Pontius Pilate. I believe and confess and utter according to the credence delivered by the Fathers who convened in the city of Nicaea and which was confirmed and supported by the Saintly Fathers in the Council of Ephesus, and if any believes in another faith than this, I condemn him according to their ordinance.

The Third Letter of Cyril to Nestorius

To Nestorius, most religious, and most dear to God, our fellow minister, Cyril, and the synod assembled at Alexandria from the province of Egypt, send greeting in the Lord.

When our Savior says in plain terms, "He that loveth father or mother more than me is not worthy of me, and he that loveth son or daughter more than me is not worthy of me," what should be our feelings who are asked by your religiousness to love you more than Christ, our common Savior? Who shall be able to succour us in the day of judgment, or what apology shall we find for our so-long silence under your blasphemies against Him? If indeed it were only yourself whom you were injuring in holding and teaching such things, it would be of less consequence, but seeing that you have given offence to the universal

Church, and have cast the leaven of a novel and strange heresy among the laity, and not the laity at Constantinople only but everywhere (for copies of your sermons have been circulated), what satisfactory account can any longer be given of our silence, or how are we not bound to remember Christ's words "Think not that I am come to send peace on the earth; I did not come to send peace but a sword; for I have come to set a man against his father, and a daughter against her mother"? For when the faith is being tampered with, perish reverence for parents as a thing unseasonable and pregnant with mischief, and let the law of natural affection to children and brethren be set aside, and let religious men count death better than life, that, as it is written, "they may obtain a better resurrection."

Take notice then that in conjunction with the holy synod that was assembled in great Rome, under the presidency of our most pious and religious brother and fellow-minister, Bishop Coelestine, we conjure and counsel you, in this third letter also, to abstain from these mischievous and perverse doctrines, which you both hold and teach, and to adopt in place of them the correct faith delivered to the Churches from the beginning by the holy Apostles and Evangelists, "who were both ministers and eyewitnesses of the Word." And unless Your Religiousness does this by the time prescribed in the epistle of our aforementioned, most pious and religious brother and fellow minister Coelestine, bishop of the Romans, know that you have neither part nor lot with us, nor place nor rank among the priests and bishops of God. For it is impossible that we should bear to see the Churches thus thrown into confusion, and the laity scandalized, and the correct faith set aside, and the flocks scattered abroad by you who ought rather to save them, if you were, as we are, a lover of correct doctrine, treading in the pious footsteps of the holy

56

Fathers. But with all, both laity and clergy, who have been excommunicated or deposed for faith's sake by your religiousness, we all are in communion. For it is not just that those who hold the true faith should be wronged by your sentence, for having rightly withstood you. For this same thing you signified in your letter to our most holy fellow bishop Coelestine, bishop of great Rome.

Following in every particular the confessions of the holy Fathers, which they have drawn up under the guidance of the Holy Spirit speaking in them, and keeping close to the meaning that they had in view, and journeying, so to speak, along the king's highway, we affirm that the very only-begotten Word of God, begotten of the very substance of the Father, true God of true God, Light that is from Light by whom all things were made, both in heaven and on earth, for our salvation came down, and of His condescension emptied Himself, and became Incarnate and was made man, that is, having taken flesh of the Holy Virgin, and made it His own from the womb, He vouchsafed to be born as we, and proceeded forth, a human being from a woman, not having cast away what He was, but even in the assumption of flesh and blood, still continuing what He was:

God in nature and truth. Neither do we say that the flesh was converted into the divine nature, nor surely that the ineffable nature of God the Word was debased and perverted into the nature of flesh, for He is unchangeable and unalterable, ever continuing altogether the same according to the Scriptures; but we say that the Son of God, while visible to the eyes, and a babe and in swaddling clothes, and still at the breast of His Virgin Mother, filled all creation as God and was seated with His Father. For the Divinity is without quantity and without magnitude and without limit.

Confessing then the personal union of the Word with

the flesh, we worship one Son and Lord, Jesus Christ, neither putting apart and sundering man and God, as though they were connected with one another by a unity of dignity and authority (for this is vain babbling and nothing else), nor surely calling the Word of God Christ in one sense, and in like manner Him who is of the woman Christ in another sense, but knowing only one Christ, the Word, which is of God the Father with His own flesh. For then [when He took flesh] He was anointed with us as man, while yet to those who are worthy to receive it Himself gives the Holy Spirit, and "not by measure," as says the blessed Evangelist John.

But neither again do we say that the Word that is of God dwelt in He who was born of the Holy Virgin as in an ordinary man, lest Christ should be understood to be a man who carries God within him, for though the Word "dwelt in us," and, as it is said, "all the fullness of the Godhead dwelt in Christ Bodily," yet we understand that when He became flesh the indwelling was not in the same manner as when He is said to dwell in the saints, but that having been united by a union of natures and not converted into flesh, He brought to pass such an indwelling as the soul of man may be said to have with its own body.

There is then one Christ, and Son and Lord, not as though He were a man possessing a conjuction with God simply by a unity of dignity or authority, for equality of honor does not unite natures.

Peter and John are equal in honor in that they are apostles and holy disciples, but the two are not one [person].

Nor certainly do we understand the mode of conjunction to be that of juxtaposition, for this does not suffice to express a union of natures.

Nor do we understand the union to be in the way of

relative participation as we, "being joined to the Lord," as it is written, "are one spirit with Him," but rather we reject the term "conjunction" altogether, as insufficient to signify the union.

Nor do we call the Word that is of God the Father the God or Master of Christ, lest we should again openly divide the one Christ and Son and Lord into two and incur the charge of blasphemy, by making Him the God and Master of Himself. For the Word of God being personally united with flesh, as we said, is God of the universe and Master of the whole world. Neither is He His own servant or His own Master for it is silly, or rather impious, to hold or say this. He did indeed speak of God as his own Father, though yet himself God by nature, and his Father's essence. But we are not ignorant, that while he continued God, he also became man subject under God, as befits the law of man's nature. But how could He become the God or Master of Himself? Therefore as man, and as befits the measure of His emptying, He speaks of Himself as subject under God with us. So also He became under the Law, though as God Himself spake the Law, and is the Lawgiver.

We refuse also to say of Christ, "For the sake of Him who assumes I worship Him who is assumed, for the sake of Him who is unseen I worship Him who is seen." One must shudder also to say, "He that is assumed shares the name of God with Him who assumed." For he who speaks again makes two Christs, one God and one man. For he confessedly denies the union according to which there is understood one Christ Jesus—not one jointly worshipped with another or jointly sharing the name of God with another, but one Christ Jesus, one only begotten Son, honored with one worship with His own flesh.

We confess also that the very Son, which was begotten

of God the Father, and is the only-begotten God, though being in His own nature impassible, suffered for us in the flesh, according to the Scriptures, and was in His crucified body impassibly appropriating and making His own the sufferings of His own flesh. And "by the grace of God He tasted death also for every man," yielding to death His own body, though originally and by nature Life, and Himself the Resurrection. For "He tasted death for every man," as I said, and returned to life again on the third day, bringing with Him the spoils of Hell, that having trampled upon death by His ineffable power, He might in His own flesh first become "the first-born from the dead", and the "first fruits of them that sleep" and might prepare the way for the return of man's nature to immortality. So that, though it be said, by "man came the resurrection of the dead," yet by "man" we understand the Word that was begotten of God and that by Him has the dominion of death been destroyed. And He will come at the appointed time, as one Son and Lord, in the glory of the Father, to judge the "world in righteousness," as it is written. And we must add this also. For showing forth the death in the flesh of the only-begotten Son of God, that is, of Jesus Christ, and confessing His return to life from the dead, and His assumption into heaven, we celebrate the service of bloodless sacrifice in the churches, and so approach the mystic benedictions, and are sanctified, being made partakers of the holy flesh and precious blood of Christ the Savior of us all, receiving it not as ordinary flesh, God forbid, nor as the flesh of a man sanctified and associated with the Word by a unity of dignity, or as having God dwelling in Him, but as life-giving of a truth and the very own flesh of the Word Himself. For being, as God, life by nature, when He became one with His own flesh, He made that flesh life-giving. So that though He says to us, "Verily,

verily I say unto you, Except ye eat the flesh of the Son of Man and drink His blood," yet we shall not account it as though it were the flesh of an ordinary man (for how could the flesh of a man give of its own nature?) but as having become of a truth the own flesh of Him, who for our sakes became and was called Son of man.

Moreover, we do not distribute the Words of our Savior in the Gospels to two several subsistence or Persons. For the one and sole Christ is not twofold, although we conceive of Him as consisting of two distinct elements inseparably united, even as a man is conceived of as consisting of soul and body, and yet is not two-fold but one out of both. But if we hold the right faith we shall believe both the human language and the Divine to have been used by one person. To one Person, therefore, must be attributed all the expressions used in the Gospels, the one Incarnate "hypostasis" of the Word, for the Lord Jesus Christ is one according to the Scriptures. And if He be called also "Apostle and High-Priest of our confession," as ministering to God the Father the confession of faith that is offered from us both to Him and through Him to God the Father, and assuredly to the Holy Spirit also, again we aver that He is by nature the only-begotten Son of God, and we do not attribute the priesthood, name and thing, to another man beside Him. For He is become a mediator between God and man, and a reconciler unto peace, having offered up Himself for a smell of a sweet savor to God the Father. For this cause also He said, "Sacrifice and offering thou wouldest not. In whole burnt offerings and sacrifices for sin thou hadst no pleasure, but a body thou hast prepared for me. Then said I, "Lo, I come. In the volume of the book it is written of me, to do thy will, O God." For He hath offered His own body for a sweet-smelling savor for us, and not for Himself. For what offering or sacrifice did He need for Himself, being as God above all sin? For though "all have sinned and do come short of the glory of God," even as we are prone to turn aside, and man's nature is diseased with the disease of sin (it is not so with Him) and failed, therefore, of His glory, how could any doubt remain that the true Lamb of God has been slain on our account and in our behalf? Saying that "He offered Himself both for Himself and for us" is nothing short of blasphemy. For in nothing was He an offender or a sinner. Of what offering then did He stand in need, there being no sin for which offering should be made with any show of reason?

And when He says of the Spirit, He "shall glorify Me," if we understand the words rightly, we shall not say that the one Christ and Son received glory from the Holy Ghost, as being in need of glory from another, for the Holy Ghost is not superior to Him and above Him. But since for the manifestation of his Godhead, He made use of the Holy Ghost for the working of miracles, He says that "He was glorified by Him," just as any one of us might say, of his strength, for instance, or his skill in any matter, "they shall glorify me." For though the Holy Spirit has a personal existence of His own and is conceived of by Himself, in that He is the Spirit and not the Son, yet He is not therefore alien from the Son. For He is called "the Spirit of Truth," and Christ is "the Truth," and He is poured forth from Him just as He is also from God the Father.

For this cause, the Holy Ghost glorified Him when He wrought miracles by the hands of the holy apostles also, after our Lord Jesus Christ had gone up to heaven. For Himself working miracles by His own Spirit, He was believed to be God by nature. For which reason also He said, He "shall take of mine and shall show it unto you." On the other hand, we do not say for a moment that the Holy

Spirit is wise and powerful by participation. For He is perfect in every respect, and wanting of no possible good. But since He is the Spirit of the Father's Power and Wisdom, that is, of the Son's, He is in very deed Wisdom and Power Himself.

But since the Holy Virgin brought forth after the flesh God personally united to flesh, for this reason we say of Her that she is "Theotokos," not as though the nature of the Word had its beginning of being from the flesh, for He was "in the beginning," and "the Word was God, and the Word was with God," and He is the Maker of the worlds, coeternal with the Father, and the Creator of the universe, but, as we said before, because having personally united man's nature to Himself, He vouchsafed also to be born in the flesh, from Her womb. Not that He needed of necessity, or for His own nature, to be born in time and in the last ages of the world, but that He might bless the very first element of our being, and that, a woman having borne Him united to flesh, there might be made to cease thenceforward the curse lying upon our whole race, which sends to death our bodies, which are of the earth, and that the sentence "In sorrow shalt thou bring forth children" being annulled by him, the words of the Prophet might be verified: "Death prevailed and swallowed up, and then again God wiped away every tear from every face." For this cause we affirm also that He blessed marriage in accordance with the dispensation by which he became man and went with His holy apostles to a marriage feast when invited at Cana of Galilee.

To these things we have been taught to assent by the holy apostles and evangelists, and by all the inspired Scriptures, and from the true confession of the blessed Fathers. To all of them it behoves Thy religiousness also to assent and consent without dissimulation of any sort.

Now the statements that Your Religiousness must anathematize are subjoined to this letter of ours.

If anyone does not confess Emmanuel to be very God, and does not acknowledge the Holy Virgin consequently to be "Theotokos," for She brought forth after the flesh, the Word of God become flesh, let him be anathema.

If anyone does not confess that the Word which is of God the Father has been personally united to flesh, and is one Christ with His own flesh, the same [person] being God and man alike, let him be anathema.

If anyone in the one Christ divides the personalities, i.e., the human and the Divine, after the union, connecting them only by a connection of dignity or authority or rule, and not rather by a union of natures, let him be anathema.

If anyone distributes to two Persons or Subsistences the expressions used both in the Gospels and in the Epistles, or used of Christ by the Saints, or by him or himself, attributing some to a man conceived of separately, apart from the Word which is of God, and attributing others, as befitting God, exclusively to the Word which is of God the Father, let him be anathema.

If anyone dares to say that Christ is a man who carries God (within Him), and not rather that He is God in truth, as one Son even by nature, even as the Word became "partaker in like manner as ourselves of blood and flesh," let him be anathema.

If anyone dares to say that the Word which is of God the Father is the God or Master of Christ, and does not. rather confess the same to be both God and man alike, the Word having become flesh according to the Scriptures, let him be anathema.

If anyone says that Jesus as a man was actuated by God the Word, and that He was invested with the glory of the only-begotten, as being other than Him let him be anathema.

If anyone dares to say that the man who was assumed ought to be worshipped jointly with God the Word, and glorified jointly, and ought jointly to share the name of God, as one in another (for the word *jointly*, which is always added, obliges one to understand this), and does not rather honor Emmanuel with one worship and offer to Him one ascription of Glory, inasmuch as the Word has become flesh, let him be anathema.

If anyone says that the one Lord, Jesus Christ, was glorified by the Spirit, as though the power that He exercised was another's received through the Spirit and not His own, and that He received from the Spirit the power of countervailing unclean spirits and of working divine miracles upon men, and does not rather say that it was His own Spirit by whom He wrought divine miracles, let him be anathema.

Divine Scripture says that Christ became "High Priest and Apostle of our confession" and that He "offered up Himself for us for a sweet-smelling savor to God the Father." If then anyone says that it was not the very Word of God Himself who became our High-Priest and Apostle when He became flesh and man as we, but another than He, and distinct from Him, a man born of a woman, or if anyone says that He offered the sacrifice for Himself also, and not rather for us alone, for He who knew no sin had no need of offering, let him be anathema.

If anyone does not confess that the Lord's flesh is life-giving and that it is the own flesh of the Word of God the Father, but affirms that it is the flesh of another than He, connected with Him by dignity, or as having only a Divine indwelling, and not rather, as we said, that it is life-giving, because it has become the own flesh of the Word who is able to quicken all things, let him be anathema.

If anyone does not confess that the Word of God suffered in the flesh and was crucified in the flesh and tasted death in the flesh and became "the first-born from the dead," even as He is both Life and Life-giving, as God, let him be anathema.

From Dioscorus to the God-loving Domnus, Bishop of Antioch

I am overwhelmed by the book of the Lord where it calls: "if it be possible, as much as lieth in you, live peaceably with all men," and I truly marvel, O God-loving, how I decided to be in peace with those who hate peace, as I have been educated by the graceful Psalmist, so it was firmly established in my conscience everlastingly; if people were to assail me, my soul transcends and I refrain from assailing them in return. Even if they tried to harm me and executed that already, I would not be bothered. As to threats of assailment, this is not my character. These are petty matters and can be tolerated as unworthy of interest. All my worry is to declare that Christ is the only begotten son of God, in Him and in His hands lies everything, for us, He was Incarnate. Absolutely, not even the slightest change occurred to him.

Those with the knowledge extinguished in their consciences and were promoted to the high offices with peccable beliefs, boastful of heresies and blasphemies, had descended with the deepest mystery of the Lord's acts to unsuitable standards. Shocked, I stand and say, "No, no, I cannot be lenient with them." I am encountering them with the words of the wise as my guidance: "to everything there is a season. A time of war, and a time of peace, a time to work and a time of zeal for the Lord." Paul has bristled the arms of the Lord, and he is calling upon us to labor. How short and how insignificant is the day! It does

66

not suffice, my writing and announcing the teachings of the men of God. They are calling upon us to rise up and reject strongly those who hate God.

It is the suitable time now to reveal the reasons that brought me to write you this letter. They say, and I do trust their word, that very many of the zealous people who believe in Christ are exposed to the storms of doubts. To deepen the sorrow, those who were supposed to manage the issues with wisdom and to calm the stirred-up storm are instigating the whirlwind of doubts and the winds of evil; they are infusing the poisons of Nestorius and would not hesitate to instill it in the body of the Church. After they have agreed with the Fathers at the holy ecumenical council in Nicaea and joined its counterpart convened in Ephesus, and after they excommunicated the rapacious beast, the enemy of Christ [Nestorius] and his misleading, I say it is truly painful that they convert so easily to poisonous arrows. They demolished that deceiving wall,[23] then reverted and erected its pillars anew. They do not have the clear conscience to come back to their senses and admit: if we resumed building what we have demolished, we are defying the laws of God. They do not conceive their ecclesiastical duties and do not value the teachings they have received, and they do not perceive that their actions are despicable and is worthy of contempt.

In the church of Antioch, the great city, where the massive population is gathered, some of those [Nestorianizers] preach blasphemies and infuse venoms, which hand can heal the ears of the hearers? Does that not evoke pity and sadness? Where people ask for cure and sympathy, they are given venom and defeat. I trust you, Most Pious, can grant these souls the healing by offering them the cure through word and labor.

It is perplexing to see the cynics preaching heresies

in the ears of the masses of believers gathered around you, of spiritual reverence.

I know the sagacious bishop of Cyrrhos to be sheltered with wisdom especially that he is near to you. O! he divides Emmanuel when he claims the Incarnate was just a human or an ordinary human was Incarnate or that without perceiving that, Thomas bowed to him as a true God. He does not instill these dogmas from his lips, but from the depth of his heart. Let him know, it is written, the time closed in to declare it loudly so I say: How far did you reach? You followed the course of blasphemy and deviated from the right path. Refrain from opposing the holy books, veil and curb your mouth, be ashamed of the voice of the Father coming down from heaven: "Thou art my beloved son, in whom I am well pleased." Do not divide into two the one Lord Jesus Christ, even though He became flesh from Saint Mary, yet when He took the body with the rational soul, He remained God as He is. Listen to Paul the philosopher asking you: "Was Christ divided?" What would be your answer when you do not believe except in two Sons, two Christs and two Lords. The prophet would shock and curb you, saying, "Here is our Lord, and we do not pursue another." He has the path of all knowledge and gave it to His servant Jacob and Israel whom He loved; later He came to earth and was accompanied by humans. Therefore the Holy Virgin is called the *Theotokos*. How marvelous what the evangelist[24] wrote: "And the Word was made flesh, and dwelt among us." He who is worshipped by the Cherubim and bowed to by the Seraphim. He Himself became like us for our sake and sat on an ass's colt and was struck by one of the officers for the sake of truth and to complete all the righteousness. This what we have been taught by those who witnessed and served the Word in the beginning. And these are the teachings of the two councils, the old[25] and the new,[26] which were also supported by John of happy memory who was a bishop before you, Most Pious.

Now I come back to you, O Christ-loving bishop of Antioch, my brother, observe that John[27] did not spare any effort to strengthen the unity of the Church at your end and ours. A unity that they cannot disrupt, they dispatched their forces against it, and without feeling it, they were about to destroy the time of peace. How glorious in the time of peace!

They are issuing sanctified writings claiming they contradict what has been written by his beatitude, our father, the famous bishop Cyril I. However, their writings were a failure and did not match the holy verses of the Lord. Our glorious father wrote so genuinely and deeply more, than any other author, and this is clear to the whole world. He was not only wise and eloquent, even though he shrouded his writings in a veil of beautiful clarity, but he also explained the mystery of the Incarnation of the Son of God with the right interpretations aided and enriched by the strength of the revelation that descended upon Him from heaven. Everything in his writings is marvelous and glorious, whether a book, a tome, an interpretation, a homily, a chapter, or an anathema;[28] indeed, he was glorious and radiating and adhering to the holy verses of God. In this instance, we have to mention: "who is the wise, and he shall understand these things? prudent, and he shall know them? for the ways of the Lord are right, and the just shall walk in them: but the transgressors shall fall therein."

Anxiety multiplies and hits the Christians to the very core; there are people[29] who set it ablaze and inflame it according to their tendencies. They extinguish the strength of the Orthodox and drive them to seas of agony. They coerce them[30] to stillness, thence conversion; this is what they want for them.

The power of labor faded away, and the norm of life is unsettled.

And those whom the lord commanded, "Go ye therefore, and teach all nations" ceased to endeavor to do so, and instead they are preaching blasphemies, and God *rebukes* the discourser: "Silence! Hold your tongue" It is written in the Bible: "If thou hast done foolishly in lifting up thyself or if thou hast thought evil, lay thine hand upon thy mouth?" This handicaps our efforts, in addition to the unsanctified words preached into our Egyptian society.

I found it my duty to write you, O Chosen by God, with brotherly friendliness and love, to let you know of all things, especially those that would promote the Christian dignity and exact the glorious churches of Christ.

Our Christ-loving king, Theodosius, who is the spring of running piety, had decided to make known his orders, which will invigorate the world and fill it with elation and joy and said his clear word in the writings of Nestorius and those who share their ideas and dogmas and oppose what has been decreed by the only two great councils, the Council of Nicaea and the Council of Ephesus. He also gave a fair judgment on the heretic Irenaous, who is biased to the destructive dogmas of Nestorius, and removed that God-void man from the bishopric of Tyre to exile, and delivered it from he who threatened the parish. And order that allurement should come to this parish through a priest who can preach the word of truth and heal the parish people, the people who were cannibalized by the beast and fell in the hands of the blasphemers, and succumbed to the evil will of an insincere shepherd. Too many of them have fallen in perplexity, and until now we did not know anything about them.

70

They[31] have mentioned your grace without praise, and they are worried that negligence may lead them to the uneven way of the wolves. This path that was not chosen by God, and we cannot reconcile with, I am afraid that a forest of poison would grow there and heighten up and push many into evil fate.

As for me, I do not think that you, Most Pious, are void of wisdom. As I know, you listen to the call of the brothers and accept their pleads to raise up to block the mouth uttering evil on God. I ask you to admonish the Orthodox and allow them to toss the silver to the money changers, and look after the parish of Tyre and grant it, by laying your hands on the bishop they choose. This you grant them by the authority given to you from God.

O God-loving, we will join your toil if it were truthful. Verily, if a number is glorified, then all members are glorified and vice versa. I ask you to consider the mutual friendship and love between us in Christ.

Our dear priests Isaiah and Korah will deliver to you this message and now will be happy when both meet you, and there is no doubt you will remember us and pray for our sake.

The Letter of Domnus to Dioscorus

To the graceful Saint Dioscorus, bishop of the great city Rakotis, from Domnus, to the God-loving Saint, our brother and apostolic brother Dioscorus

O God-loving, have read Your Holiness' letter, embracing phrases of love to us, which shows your spiritual nobility. O God-pious, as you certainly know the agreement between the pious bishops of the East[32] on theological dogmas that were canonized by the Saintly Fathers con-

71

gregated in Nicaea. Several tomes from many were sent, on several occasions, and addressed to you in the time of the graceful bishop Cyril I of happy memory, and of us less value is what we have written now by the hand of the pious priest Osieb. As for those who speak not the truth, are obliged to learn from Your Holiness how to succumb to the faith decreed by the Saintly Fathers in Nicaea and universally accepted and supported by the holy bishops' council convened in Ephesus I. They observed with esteem and appreciation what was written by John of happy memory who led the Church before us, on issues where he explained the faith according to the right dogma. Similarly the tome written by the wholly blessed Athanasius to his beatitude Epictetus. We have made every effort to affirm these beliefs in people's minds. We would have not done that unless we are firmly holding to it as we hold to the absolute truth, and we worked to spread and support it. As for those who are not asserted in peace and tend to feud, not only . . . [33]

. . . in all that concerns God, rude tongues are to be shut and those who were deceived with these petty matters are demanded not to pay attention to the said lies. With regard to the Church of God in Tyre, we have spoken as possible about it with the pious and righteous and the priests, with whom we were happy. With their deep wisdom to meet with them and in that our clergy shares, too. We are proud of your ascending to the throne, O Saint, and your two messengers will relate that to you. We beg Your Holiness to pray for our sake and to delight us with your writings and those of the brothers with you. Myself and those with me greet you.

The Second Letter of Dioscorus

From Dioscorus to Archbishop Domnus of Antioch

When problems turn acute and tragedies accumulate, evoking deep sadness in the soul, a human may submit to absolute silence and complete perplexity because of a slumbering thought that does not know how to wake up. We have to keep ourselves away from that, lest we should be found guilty of evil.

I always wish to write in love and peace and receive in return the same. And this is my wish to the churches crowned with complete unity, enjoying one faith. Maybe I am asking for what is difficult to reach. I am saying it because things demand traveling on a long, difficult path, steep with many slippery routes. It seems we cannot travel except in this path, even in the easy, simple matters. If the danger is imminent even in the straight path, then how will we be spared of sin if our silence is not in its place? We need to say together with the wise Paul, "Who shall separate us from the love of Christ? Shall tribulation or distress, or persecution, or famine, or nakedness, or peril, or the sword? As it is written for thy sake, we are killed all the day long; we are accounted as sheep for the slaughter."

Since I believe in this way and hold to this teaching, I am writing to you, O God-loving, asking to direct those known preachers who are there to the true faith, those who may think they are uttering the true teachings, as they are convinced they are right, but be confident that they bewilder many. It is pitiful they neither know what they say nor what they speak of.

The Church looks upon you, O pious; prepare a bridle and a halter to curb the mouths of those who do not know

God. They claim that Nestorius the blasphemer was unfairly excommunicated without deviating from the right path and without injuring Christ. They do not admit that he instilled heresies in the Orthodox faith that is derived from the Bible. And they claim that he scorned to attend the holy ecumenical council that by the will of God convened in Ephesus and disdained to join the meeting in which the saintly beatitude[34] was in. I tell them: Be ye not unequally yoked together with unbelievers: for what fellowship hath righteousness with unrighteousness? and what communions hath light with darkness? And what concern hath Christ with Belial? or what part hath he that believeth with an infidel?

But what made him evade the congregation, even though the council invited him, was his fear that his conscience would severely scold him. How true are the words "the evil escapes, and there is no chaser." And there was another factor that made him avoid meeting with the Saintly Fathers of the Orthodox faith, that is, because he was an unbeliever. If he was adopting a true dogma, he would have attended the council so that his belief would shine among the Fathers, to whom the Lord's word applies: "For where two or three are gathered together in my name there am I in the midst of them." If two or three gathered for the sake of righteousness, truly Christ will be among them, as for those who are afraid of attending such a gathering will have no share in it. How then not ashamed are they who try to belittle this holy council convened in Ephesus[35] and try to isolate it from the council of Nicaea, while both are one in aim? Both were convened for the sake of Christ's name. The first expelled Arius and the second Nestorius. The first eradicated blasphemy from earth, and the second supported the canons of the first. . . . [36]

. . . it rebukes those who are on the side of blasphemy; therefore, I do not know how uncertainty prevailed in the churches. This is not only from those who are in the East, but also from the righteous monks we have here, who traveled back and forth in the East. They traveled between the monasteries of Alexandria preaching these teachings among those who escaped from the cobweb of this world.[37] Those are in perplexity and uneasiness and they claim; he who caused this bewilderment should be handed over to God's judgment. Observe your beatitude, in which seas we are lost, and what should we do to settle these matters.

We hope you will read our message in a public congregation. If someone is bewildering any of these young ones, deserves a severe judgment, then what a grave ending awaits he who involves all those monks in this stormy sea of bewilderment! But we should have faith in the Lord; He is able to end these doubts and unsettlement. In Him we live, move, and have our being.

The First Letter of Saint Dioscorus to His Monks

I know Him, and with faith I transcend. He was born God of the Father, and I know Him to be born man from the Virgin. I see Him walking as a man on earth and behold Him to heavenly angels as God. I envisage Him sleeping in the ship as a man and He Himself walks on the water as God. As a human He experiences hunger, and as God, He feeds. He, as human, was stoned by the Jews, and He Himself is worshipped by the angels as God. He was tempted as a human, but expells devils as God. Many such examples could be cited, however, to avoid controversies, I shall not continue quoting the many [Biblical] verses that

75

support these two facts. God willing, I shall speak of it on a more suitable occasion.

I confess He is one; while He Himself is God and Savior, He became man because of His goodness. Furthermore, I will ignore those who deny that. Hold to the faith of the Fathers and do not heed the teachings of the blasphemers as they corrupt souls, nor to those who divide the one into two. Our Savior is one as I have said; however, He became man because of His kindness. With their true teachings the Saintly Orthodox Fathers have rebuked the heretics and declared that confession of two natures of the Incarnate Word is a heresy and condemned those who dare and believe in that. Those who did not acknowledge the Divine Logos and that in the fullness of time He who is consubstantial with the Father has become human without change for our salvation and that when He became the son with human nature, He (Divinity) did not change were considered (by the Fathers) estranged from the Christian's hope, as they considered the rest of the heretics.

To put across the correct doctrine founded on the rock of the Orthodox faith and to ridicule the said heresies, I quote the inspired Biblical verses. He is the body born from the Virgin with a rational soul, thus absolutely condemning all heresies, therefore affirming the Orthodox faith repleted with joy and delivered to us by the saintly apostles and the trustworthy Fathers. This for those who deny the Lord to hear and repent according to the verse.

The Second Letter of Saint Dioscorus to His Monks

I will not comment on many important issues for the time being; however, I declare the following:

No one dare say that the Holy body taken from the

Virgin by Our Lord is not consubstantial with ours, as it is known, and as it is so. Thus those who claim that Christ did not take our body are contradicting Paul's verse: "For verily He took not on Him the nature of angels; but He took on Him the seed of Ibraham." As Saint Mary was not alien to him[38] and according to the Bible wherefore in all things it behoved Him to be made like unto His brethren. The statement "made like unto His brethren" affirms that He has not taken part of our nature, but He has taken all. In brief, He has taken all our body, including the rational soul. It is the body delivered by Saint Mary with a rational soul without a man's involvement. If the issues were different, as the heretics claim, how was He called our brother? If He has taken a body alien to ours, how then could it be true what He told His Father: "I will declare thy name unto My brethren"? We have to refuse those who deny that He became consubstantial with our nature for our salvation. He dwelt among us, not a shadow or an illusion as claimed by the followers of the heresy of Mani, but He was truly born from Mary the Theotokos to revive us because of His goodness and to mend the container that was broken in us and renew it. He is Emmanuel who appeared poor for our sake, according to Paul," to obtain richness in His lowliness. According to His own will He became like us so in His grace we can be like Him. He became man and still the Son of God so we can be the children of God by His grace."

This is my dogma and what I believe in. If someone does not believe in that, then he is strange to the apostles' faith.

Notes

1. In rare circumstances, this dangerous intermingling of the spiritual authority and the civil executive power did take place. When King Akhenaten (1387–66 B.C.) started his religious reform by calling for the one God, Aton, he alienated the powerful priests of Amun Temple. Later, Akhenaten was forced to move the capital to Akhenaten (Tel el Amarna).

2. This is obvious in Mr. Sadat's own writings, where we can see clearly the factors that helped the shaping of his personality. In his Book (*In Search of Identity*, New York: Harper and Row, 1977, pp. 5–6), Mr. Sadat wrote: "But the ballad which affected me most deeply was probably that of Zahran, the hero of Denshway, I recall listening to my mother reciting it to me as I lay stretched out on the top of our huge rustic oven, half-asleep, while my younger brothers, as well our rabbits, had fallen asleep. . . . I listened to that ballad night after night, half-awake, half-asleep, which perhaps made the story sink in my subconscious. My imagination roamed free. I often saw Zahran and lived his heroism in dream and reverie. I wished I were Zahran." Mr. Kissinger recognised the dreaming unrealistic element in Mr. Sadat's personality. According to Mr. Sadat (p. 228), Mr. Kissinger's advice to Sadat was " . . . be realistic. We live in real world and cannot build anything on fancies and wishful thinking."

Most incredible was Mr. Sadat's answer to a question put to him in an interview for Danish television (published in leading Egyptian newspapers November 26, 1980):

Q: Sir, Can you comment on the claim that you are studying at the moment taking a political resolution that will be the decision of 1980?
A: Important decisions on that level are not prepared at all. These [decisions] are latent in my mind. They will come out whenever situations necessitate. They are concealed in my subconscious and will come out whenever conditions are favorable.

Did Mr. Sadat know that: In a neurosis, the conflict between instinct and resistance, due to a particular objectionable impulse, is repressed, with the impulse retaining its full charge of energy? Accordingly, the ego is obliged to protect itself against the constant threat of renewed advance on the part of the repressed impulse by making a permanent expenditure of energy, a countercharge. Now the repressed impulse became unconscious and is able to find means of discharge via the nervous supply of the body to produce symptoms (Sigmund Freud, *An Autobiographical Study*, London: The Hogarth Press, 1950, pp. 50–70). Thus, objectional impulses, and not important political decisions, can become unconscious. Psychoanalysis can reveal to the consciousness the repressed impulse, thereby withdrawing the charge from it and eliminating the symptoms.

Mr. Sadat wanted to instill fear in the heart of the Egyptians, e.g., the 1981 political purge of liberals, secular politicians, and Pope Shenoudah III, and at the same time he demanded absolute respect and love from his sons and children! Poor Sadat! He was incapable of forgetting the experience of his early childhood. The following quote from his book (p. 7) is self-explanatory: "I remember how in the spring my friends and I lingered by the palace [of King Fuad] to pick a few apricots, though in fear and trepidation; indeed to touch anything belonging to the king could spell death. I could never known then that I would grow up to take part, with a number of my colleagues, in changing the course of history—that I myself would one day cross that awesome wall and sit on the very chair on which King Fuad, and subsequently King Farouk, had sat."

Furthermore, in his youth, Mr. Sadat demonstrated a great ability to cheat and lie, as is obvious in his book: p. 37— " . . . Working very hard on it, I had, by the end of three days, mapped out a complete story in my mind. . . ."; p. 38—" . . . I then invented a whole story about his coming to see me at Salt's in Heliopolis. . . ."; and p. 62–67—" . . . I realised that Hussein had made a clean breast of everything. He had omitted nothing, down to the minutest details, almost like a tape recorder. . . . At a hastily arranged meeting, Hussein simply reiterated his declared position while I made up a story which gave an innocuous reason for our acquaintanceship and meetings; it was completely false. . . ."

3. One can cite two examples, of the very many, to show how the Copts failed to comprehend the reality of their situation in relation to the Muslim majority and to correctly identify the different factors controlling the equilibrium of this relationship.

First, during the time of Abdul Aziz ben Marwan, John, the fortieth Pope of Alexandria, recommended that upon his death a certain pious monk by the name of Isaac be his successor. Shortly after the Pope's death in A.D. 686, several bishops conferred with some Alexandrian priests and civilian dignitaries and decided to elect Georges the Deacon as the forty-first Pope, against the will of the deceased one. The rest of the holy synod and the supporters of Isaac refused Georges. The two parties were unable to reconcile their differences and therefore went to Governor Abdul Aziz to decide for them! Abdul Aziz favored Isaac, who was consequently consecrated as Pope Isaac the forty-first of Alexandria. Georges did not give up and bribed the court of Abdul Aziz to influence him to change his mind. However, his scheme did not work (Deacon Manasa El Komous, *Book of the History of the Coptic Church*, Cairo: Yakazah Press, 1924, pp. 386–87)

The incident in itself is surprising. The Copts should have realized that the new establishment was not headed by Emperor Constantine and his successors, but rather by governors of a different religion.

Second, the Copts of today repeated the same mistake:

a. In 1955, Coptic laymen asked the government of Colonel Nasser to remove Pope Yusab II from office! (E. Wakin, *A Lonely Minority: The Modern Story of Egypt's Copts*, New York: William Morrow and Company, 1963.)

b. There are strong indications that the late Bishop John of Giza had submitted a request to the government of Mr. Nasser to remove Pope Cyril VI (1959–71) from the chair of Saint Mark!

c. Again, the Copts failed to understand that the colonels of the 1952 coup d'etat converted the secular society governed by the former liberal politicians of the Wafd party into a military society with a corrupt judicial system, especially during the years of Mr. Sadat's governments. Therefore, it was not surprising at all that the government lawyer Gamal Laban declared on April 13, 1983, that: "That court has simply upheld the decision to depose the Pope [His Holiness Shenoudah III] and dissolve the five-man papal committee. The decision means an acting Pope must then be elected to run the affairs of the church until the election of a new one."

Paradoxically, the Copts, who resented Mr. Sadat's move against His Holiness Pope Shenoudah III, entrusted the whole issue to the hand of corrupt jurisdiction manipulated by the government, which resulted in further complications. The most rational approach to solve this national impasse could have been accomplished in two ways:

a. The government-appointed committee of five bishops (September 5, 1981) could have taken a low profile in managing the affairs of the church under the supervision of the exiled Pope, or

b. Leading Coptic civilians could have synchronized their efforts with

Muslim liberals to clarify this problem in the mind of the Egyptian population, namely that Pope Shenoudah was protecting the rights of the See of Alexandria from the tyranny of the corrupt political system of Mr. Sadat.

Thus enough momentum could have been gathered to force the government into seriously reconsidering its position.

4. During this period, Alexandria was called by its ancient Egyptian name, Rakotis.

5. The Acts of the Ephesian Council in Syriac, p. 289.

6. "The Content of the Holy Orthodox Council of Chalcedon in the Cause of the Heresy of Eutyches the Hypocrite," published (in Arabic) in Rome, 1694, by the authorization of the bishop of Rome, pp. 35, 37, and 38.

7. Ibid.

8. While defining the true orthodoxy at Ephesus I, Cyril I secured the hostility of John of Antioch until they agreed to compromise in A.D. 433.

   See J. Stevenson, *Creeds, Councils and Controversies* (London: S.P.C.K., 1978), pp. 276–89 and 290–95 and G. L. Prestige, *Fathers and Heretics* (London: S.P.C.K., 1979), pp. 156–79.

9. Some authors claimed that Archbishop Domnus of Antioch was the third president of the council, but this is doubtful in the light of his condemnation.

10. In this regard, Leo acted as if he already had the authority over the Archbishops of Rakotis, Constantinople, Antioch, and Jerusalem. It is incredulous indeed how arch-Nestorianizers such as Theodoret of Cyrrhos and Ibas of Edessa were confirmed at Chalcedon by Leo as true Orthodox to use them later to stab Dioscorus. For example, Theodoret wrote to Domnus of Antioch on the occasion of the death of Cyril-I (who is regarded as the champion of the Orthodox faith by almost every Christian) the following letter, which can be taken as an indication of the Nestorian inclinations of Theodoret and his deep hatred of Cyril I:

    . . . This wretch, however, has not been dismissed by the Ruler of our souls like other men, that he may possess for longer time the things which seem to be full of joy. Knowing that the fellow's malice has been daily growing and doing harm to the body of the Church, the Lord has lopped him off like a plague and taken away the reproach from the children of Israel. His survivors are indeed delighted at his departure. The dead, maybe, are sorry. There is some ground for alarm lest they should be so much annoyed at his company as to send him back to us, or that he should run away from his conductors like the tyrant of Cyniscus in Lucian. Great care must then be taken, and it is especially your Holiness's business to undertake this duty, to tell the guild of undertakers to lay a very big heavy stone upon his grave, for the fear he should come back again, and show his changeable mind once more. Let him take his new doctrines to the shades below, and preach to them all day and all night. We are not at all afraid of his dividing them by making public addresses against true religion and by investing an immortal nature with death. He will not be stoned only by ghosts learned in divine law, but also by Nimrod, Pharaoh, and Sennacherib, or any other of God's enemies. . . .

G. L. Prestige's comment on the above letter (Fathers and Heretics, pp. 311–12) is indeed interesting: "The authorship of the letter is not beyond all doubt, but it seems most probably that it was penned by the gentle and warmhearted Theodoret. It affords striking testimony to Cyril's greatness. Small men do not earn such heartfelt obituaries, even from deeply indignant saints."

However, we feel that it reflects a typical Theodoret jealousy of the Egyptian Cyril, especially the last statement of Theodoret posing the pharaohs as one of the enemies of God. Generally, it reflects the ignorance of Theodoret and his compatriots of the culture and civilization of the Egyptian people. The sun cult of Akhenaten was the first realization by man of a unique single power behind the creation of the universe and living substances. There is no doubt that the hymns of King Akhenaten are equivalent in importance to those of David as man's first approach to his one Creator. Monastic life in the ancient Egyptian culture is unparalled in any other culture. This is clearly manifested in the following prayer, especially related to the removal of the intestines and placing them in a chest, recited while the embalming of a deceased Egyptian (J.E. Harris and K.R. Weeks, *X-Raying of Pharaohs*, New York: Charles Scribner's Sons, pp. 87–88):

"O lord Sun and all you gods who give life to men, receive me favorably and commit me to abide with the everlasting gods.

"For as long as I continued in that life, I have steadfastly reverenced the gods whom my parents instructed me to worship, and I have ever honored those who brought my body into the world, while, as concerns my fellow men, I have done no murder nor betrayed a trust, nor committed any other bad sin.

"But if during my life, I have sinned in eating or drinking

what was unlawful, the fault was not mine but of these." (the priest shows the chest in which the stomach was.)

It is not difficult then to understand why their grandchildren, Saint Antonius, Saint Pachomius, Saint Shenouti, and many others have embarked on monastic life in Christianity, which has flourished in the Egyptian desert since then.

11. H. Chadwick, *The Early Church*, (England: Penguin Books, 1975), fn., p. 201.

12. Historically speaking, those bishops and others, including Nestorius himself, took their views on the person of Christ from Theodore of Mopsuestia, who died in 428.

13. See R. B. Betts, *Christians in the Arab East*, (Athens: Lycabettus Press, 1978); G. Every, *Understanding Eastern Christianity*, (England: S.C.M. Press Ltd., 1980); E. Lancioni, *The History of the Popes*, (New York: Manor Books, Inc., 1978); and J. Tager, *Moslems and Copts since the Arab Invasion of Egypt*, Cairo: Dar El Maaref. 1951.

14. E. L. Butcher, *The Story of the Church of Egypt*, vol. 1 (London: Smith Elder and Company, 1897.)

15. Dr. H. Chadwick argues that Flavian died in February, 450, and not in August, 449. Anatolius would have been nominated during Flavian's lifetime. Therefore, Anatolius could have had an interest in the elimination of his predecessor. So it would be quite possible that Anatolius, Leo's ally in Chalcedon, had some hand in Flavian's death on his way to exile (H. Chadwick, *The Exile and Death of Flavian of Constantinople: A Prologue to the Council of Chalcedon*, NSG, 1955, pp. 17–34).

16. Fliche and Martin, *Histoire de l'Eglise* vol. 4 p. 233.

17. Most likely the deacon Hilarus, who had his eyes fixed on the bishopric of Rome, synthesized the appeal of Flavian to Leo. In 461, Hilarus occupied the throne of Saint Peter in Rome!

18. It is known that Theophilous, one of the most powerful Popes Egypt ever had, instilled dignity and greatness in the sunken spirit of the colonized Egypt. His two successors, Cyril I and Dioscorus, were men of the same caliber who executed precisely the same policy until they had made Egypt an independent country in all but name.

19. It is amazing how history repeats itself. Although there is a wide gulf, of over 1,500 years, separating His Holiness Shenoudah III, Pope of Rakotis, and his predecessor Dioscorus, the political events that shaped their circumstances were almost identical, except that Pope Shenoudah III has cordial relations with the Catholic Church. The monk who orchestrated Mr. Sadat moves against Pope Shenoudah III is the abbot of the cloister of Saint Makarius in Wadi el-Natrun, by the name of Matta el-Meskin. Judas got the silver of Pontius Pilate, Anatolius secured the blessing of Emperor Marcian and Matta el-Meskin was

rewarded with some acres of desert land from Mr. Sadat on which to grow watermelons and beets.

20. K. Mourad, *The Civilization of Coptic Egypt* (Cairo: Dar El Alam El Arabi Press).

21. Nothing demonstrates this fact more than Nestorius' comment pertaining to the Tome of Leo: "For the bishop of Rome read what had been done against Eutyches, and he condemned Eutyches because of his impiety. As for myself, when I had found and read this writing [Tome of Leo], I thanked God that the Church of Rome had an Orthodox and irreproachable confession of faith, although in so far as concerns me, she had come to a different decision."

Thus Nestorius, in his document *Liber Heraclidis*, declared himself in agreement with the Christology of Flavian and of the Tome of Leo, i.e., confirming Nestorius' knowledge of Leo's writing. Consequently, the argument of A. Grillmeir (*Christ in Christian Tradition*, vol. 1, Atlanta: John Knox Press, 1975, p. 518) that: "As his [Nestorius'] formulas and his joyful welcome of the Tome of Leo show, he stood at the very gateway of Chalcedon. Only a little, but vital, assistance in speculative theology and the doors could have opened for him" is not surprising at all, since the Council of Chalcedon was dominated by Nestorianizers, as we have shown. We have to remember that Nestorius had caused so much scandal by his own derogatory remarks about the title "Theotokos or "Mother of God" and his statement "God is not a baby two or three months old" (H. Chadwick, *The Early Church*, London: Penguin Books, 1975, pp. 197–98). Therefore, Leo's Tome and the bishops who supported it in Chalcedon were and still are suspects in the eyes of the Cyrillian Orthodox Copts.

22. The Acts of The Holy Ephesian II Council in Syriac and *The Contents of the Holy Orthodox Council of Chalcedon in the Cause of the Heresy of Eutyches the Hypocrite*, published in Rome in 1694 by the authorization of the bishop of Rome, pp. 84 and 85.

23. Metaphor. Dioscorus was referring to demolishing "Nestorian heresies."

24. Saint John.

25. Nicaea.

26. Ephesus.

27. Predecessor of Domnus.

28. Dioscorus is pointing to the third letter of Cyril I of Rakotis.

29. Nestorianizers.

30. The Orthodox believers.

31. The priests and laymen who shared the Orthodox beliefs of Rakotis.

32. Domnus was referring to the agreement of John of Antioch and Cyril I of Rakotis.

33. At this point, the letter is worn out.

34. Cyril I of Rakotis.
35. Ephesus I.
36. At this point, the letter is worn out.
37. The monks.
38. Christ's body is consubstantial with Saint Mary's.

Index